Routledge Revivals

The Life of Jesus Christ

First published in 1955, *The Life of Jesus Christ* gives a lucid factual account of Christ's life and examines His claim to be the Messiah whose life in time and space can only be understood in the light of the eternal purposes of God. The author writes objectively from the evidence available but reminds us that the authors of the Gospels, which must be the principal sources of information, were writing from a theological point of view and had no intention of stating objective facts without any sort of interpretation. He believes that in studying the life of Christ we need a combination of faith and reason, and that two are not necessarily antagonistic. This book will be of interest to students of religion and history.

The Life of Jesus Christ

J. W. C. Wand

Routledge
Taylor & Francis Group

First published in February 3, 1955
Second edition February 1961
By Methuen & Co. Ltd.

This edition first published in 2024 by Routledge
4 Park Square, Milton Park, Abingdon, Oxon, OX14 4RN
and by Routledge
605 Third Avenue, New York, NY 10017

Routledge is an imprint of the Taylor & Francis Group, an informa business

© J. W. C. Wand, 1955 and 1961

All rights reserved. No part of this book may be reprinted or reproduced or utilised in any form or by any electronic, mechanical, or other means, now known or hereafter invented, including photocopying and recording, or in any information storage or retrieval system, without permission in writing from the publishers.

Publisher's Note
The publisher has gone to great lengths to ensure the quality of this reprint but points out that some imperfections in the original copies may be apparent.

Disclaimer
The publisher has made every effort to trace copyright holders and welcomes correspondence from those they have been unable to contact.

A Library of Congress record exists under LCCN: 55028913

ISBN: 978-1-032-73499-6 (hbk)
ISBN: 978-1-003-46450-1 (ebk)
ISBN: 978-1-032-73501-6 (pbk)

Book DOI 10.4324/9781003464501

The Life of
Jesus Christ

by

J. W. C. WAND

METHUEN & CO. LTD, LONDON
36 ESSEX STREET, STRAND, WC2

First published February 3, 1955
Second edition 1961

2.1

CATALOGUE NO. 2/4470/10

*Printed in Great Britain by
Jarrold and Sons Ltd, Norwich*

PREFACE

TO write a life of Christ is the most honourable and at the same time the most difficult task that any historian can be asked to undertake. It is the most honourable because on any reasonable estimate the personality of Jesus is the most influential that the history of mankind has ever known. It is the most difficult because so much of the evidence does not easily lend itself to ordinary historical evaluation.

While it is probable that today no reputable historian would doubt the fact that Jesus of Nazareth was crucified under Pontius Pilate, historians are by no means agreed about the factual reality of many other statements made with regard to the details of His life and work. In the last resort we frequently have to decide whether the character of Jesus is such as to make us accept in His case claims for which, if made on behalf of any other historical personage, we should certainly say there was insufficient evidence.

Further, in the documents available it is not always easy to say precisely what claim is being made. To take but one instance: in reading of the raising of Lazarus it is almost inevitable that we should ask whether this incident really occurred. Yet many of the most competent of modern commentators would tell us that this is almost the worst question we could ask, because it reveals, so they would say, a complete misunderstanding of a highly mystical and dramatic author.

In such circumstances the mood in which the reader approaches the narrative is all-important. I have tried to make it clear in the following pages that in my view we need a combination of faith and reason, and that the two are not necessarily antagonistic. I have also tried to let the gospel story speak for itself, while allowing the variations of strength and weakness in the documentary evidence to appear with sufficient clarity.

I am very grateful to the Rev G. D. Kilpatrick, Dean Ireland's Professor in the University of Oxford, who has read my manuscript and saved my unwary feet from several pitfalls. I have also to thank Dr E. V. Rieu for opening my eyes to many subtleties in the meaning of the gospel text.

✠ Wm : Londin :

PREFACE TO THE NEW EDITION

THE call for a new edition has provided the opportunity to sketch the portrait of Jesus Christ as seen by each of the evangelists independently. Such an attempt now appears as Chapter XIV. I hope the reader will find that the effort to look through the eyes of each of the evangelists in turn will give him a better knowledge of the Figure in the round.

The task of discovering a consistent chronological scheme for our Lord's ministry reminds one of the patient (and ultimately successful) research for an original design among the fragments of stained glass windows in York Minster. The former task, now given up by scholars, has been taken on by the writers of detective fiction, who have their own peculiar qualifications. I confess my own indebtedness to one of the best of them, Freeman Wills Croft, whose harmony entitled *The Four Gospels in One Story* presents us with as likely a reconstruction as any I know.

1961 ✠ Wm : Wand

CONTENTS

PREFACE   v

Chapter I
INTRODUCTORY

I. DID JESUS EXIST? *Pagan and Jewish evidence.*   2
   *Suetonius. Tacitus. Pliny. Josephus. Early
   Rabbis.*

II. CHRISTIAN SOURCES. *The Church. Paul.*   5
    *The Fourth Gospel. Synoptists. Documentary criticism. Form criticism. Difficulty
    for the biographer.*

III. FURTHER ESTIMATE. *Purpose of gospels.*   12
     *Meaning of name. Other references in N.T.
     Apocryphal gospels. Inspired prophet or
     apocalyptist? Son of Man and Son of God.*

IV. A NEW DIFFICULTY. *The meaning of myth.*   15
    *The divine in terms of the human. Need of
    the historical. Our method.*

Chapter II
EARLY YEARS

I. PRELIMINARIES. *History and scheme of*   19
   salvation. Genealogical trees. Virgin birth.

II. THE NATIVITY. *The census. The birth. The*   24
    *shepherds. The Magi. Herod and the flight
    into Egypt.*

III. NAZARETH. *Circumcision and Purification.*   29
     Boyhood at the Temple. Education.

Chapter III
ENVIRONMENT

I. PALESTINE A PALIMPSEST. *Hellenistic*   33
   *culture. Jewish dispersion—Alexandria.
   Roman law. Native princes.*

II. JEWISH PARTIES. *Herodians. Sadducees.*   36
    Elders. Pharisees. Scribes. Zealots. Essenes.

III. GEOGRAPHICAL DIVISIONS. *Samaria.* 38
Galilee. (Apocalyptists.)

IV. JUDAISM. *Better than Paganism. Converts.* 40
The special seed-plot of Christianity.

Chapter IV
BEGINNING OF THE MINISTRY

I. JESUS AT HOME. *His early manhood. The* 43
Baptist. Jesus' call.

II. JESUS' BAPTISM. *Age. Joins John's move-* 45
ment. His baptism. Fourth Gospel interpre-
tation.

III. THE TEMPTATION. *How to conduct the* 47
Messianic mission.

IV. BEGINNING OF THE MISSION. *First* 49
disciples. Galilee. First preaching. First
miracle.

Chapter V
GROWING POPULARITY

I. LENGTH OF THE MINISTRY. *Chronological* 52
arrangement. General outline.

II. FIRST YEAR. *Mainly in Galilee but two visits* 54
to Jerusalem. First visit to Jerusalem.
Nicodemus. Baptizing in Judea. Return to
Galilee. Woman at well. Nobleman's sick
son at Cana.

III. WORK IN CAPERNAUM. *Preaching from boat* 57
and call of disciples. Healing of demoniac
and of Peter's mother-in-law. Nazareth.
Sermon and rejection.

IV. JERUSALEM AGAIN. *Paralytic at Bethesda.* 59
Beginning of Jews' opposition. Imprisonment
of Baptist. Return to Capernaum. Breach
with Pharisees. Further quarrel about
Sabbath observance.

V. BEGINNING OF ORGANISATION. *Choice of* 62
Twelve. Their marching orders. Sermon on
the Plain? Centurion's servant. Widow of

Nain and her son. The Pharisee and the prostitute.

Chapter VI
THE STORY-TELLER

I. THE PARABLES. *Why they occupy so large a space. Precedents for the style.* — 68

II. COMPARISON OF STYLES. *Similes in Fourth Gospel and elsewhere. O.T. parables. The national style. In it Jesus excels.* — 69

III. INTERPRETATION. *The direct moral approach. Extended similes or allegories? One point only? Does Jesus allegorize? The Sower. The Unjust Steward.* — 73

IV. PURPOSE. *Comprehensive. Challenge of the Kingdom. Subsidiary aims. Care for the lost.* Disciplina arcani. *Nature seen to be sacramental.* — 76

Chapter VII
THE TURNING-POINT

I. THE FATE OF THE BAPTIST. *John's disciples question Jesus. Jesus' estimate of John and of Jewish apathy. The murder of John. Feeding of 5,000 and of 4,000. Culminating point.* — 79

II. TRAINING OF DISCIPLES. *Jesus walks on water. Tour with disciples. Caesarea Philippi. Peter the confessor and the rock. Prophecies of passion. Transfiguration. Failure of disciples to heal case of epilepsy.* — 82

III. FURTHER WANDERINGS IN GALILEE. *The Temple tax. Quarrels among disciples. Attitude to outsiders. Forgiveness. Journey to Jerusalem for Feast of Tabernacles. Discussion in Jerusalem.* — 88

Chapter VIII
THE TEACHER

I. JESUS' DOUBLE WORK. *Revelation and redemption. Teaching and preaching—'Gospel'. Picture of Teacher. His audiences.* — 93

No system. Law-giver, prophet, wise man, poet. Authority.

II. THE KINGDOM. *False ideas. Three aspects.* 96

III. THE CHURCH. *Mentions by Matthew. Constitution of the 'little flock'. Not an end in itself.* 99

IV. GOD. *Father of mankind, of Jesus, and of all. Jesus—Son of Man. Son of God. Suffering Servant. Redeemer (love, sin, ransom). Lamb of God, repentance, forgiveness.* 100

V. CONDUCT. *Revolutionary principle. Love. Absolute standards. (Schweitzer and interim ethics.) Two standards? A double situation.* 104

Chapter IX
THE PERIOD OF OPPOSITION

I. MISSION OF SEVENTY AND ITS RESULTS. *Breach with professional classes. Good Samaritan. Prayer. Quarrel about exorcism. Signs. Washing before meat. Division of a legacy. Rich fool. Need for decision. Be always ready.* 108

II. FEAST OF DEDICATION. *Challenge by the Jews, and threatened stoning. Jesus escapes to east of Jordan. Mere acquaintance with Messiah not enough. Pharisees warn Him to flee. Precedence at table.* 115

III. RETURN TO JERUSALEM. *Death and raising of Lazarus. Impromptu meeting of Sanhedrin. Jesus withdraws. Prophesies His end. Zacchaeus. Blind Bartimaeus. Dinner at Bethany with Simon the Leper.* 119

Chapter X
THE WONDER-WORKER

I. THE STORIES ESSENTIAL TO THE NARRATIVE. 123

CONTENTS

II. THE MOTIVE OF COMPASSION. *Revelation of the Kingdom. Not to compel belief in Kingdom or His divinity. Signs of the Kingdom.*   124

III. TERMS EMPLOYED. *Varied nature. Healing. The dead. Fact or allegory.*   126

IV. CREDIBILITY. *Do they fit the scheme of revelation? 'Miracles cannot happen.'*   128

Chapter XI
THE PASSION

SUNDAY. *Preparations and entry into Jerusalem. Visit to Temple.*   131

MONDAY. *Barren fig-tree. Cleansing of Temple. The song of the children.*   133

TUESDAY. *Discourse on the fig-tree. Questions by the Temple authorities, by the Herodians, by the Sadducees, and by the Pharisees. Three parables. Widow's farthing. Greeks wish to see Him. The rebuilding of the Temple. Discourse on the end. Three more parables.*   135

WEDNESDAY. *Woman taken in adultery. Meal at Simon's house? Caiaphas calls a meeting. Judas' betrayal.*   143

Chapter XII
THE LAST DAYS

MAUNDY THURSDAY. *Arrangements for Last Supper. The feet-washing. The Body and Blood. The discourse and the Hallel. Gethsemane. The betrayal. The arrest. Examination before Annas, before informal Sanhedrin meeting (Peter and Judas), before Pilate, Herod and Pilate again. The condemnation.*   146

GOOD FRIDAY. *Simon bears the cross. The Crucifixion. The seven words. The portents in Jerusalem. The piercing of Jesus' side.*   157

SATURDAY. *What happened to the disciples?*   161

xii THE LIFE OF JESUS CHRIST

Chapter XIII
THE TRIUMPH

I. THE RESURRECTION. *Historical event that made all the difference. The documents.* 163

II. THE WOMEN AT THE TOMB. *Peter and John. Appearance to Mary Magdalene. Appearance to women. Story invented by chief priests.* 164

III. TWO DISCIPLES AT EMMAUS. *Appearance to Peter. Appearance to disciples in upper room. Appearance to Thomas.* 166

IV. THIRD APPEARANCE TO DISCIPLES. *In Galilee by the sea. Testing of Peter. St. Matthew's version of the last charge. St. Paul's additions.* 168

V. FINAL APPEARANCE. *Ascension.* 169

Chapter XIV
FOUR PORTRAITS OF CHRIST

I. INFLUENCE OF ST. PAUL 172

II. THE MYSTERIOUS REDEEMER OF MARK 173

III. THE UNIVERSAL HERO OF LUKE 177

IV. THE PRE-ORDAINED MESSIAH OF MATTHEW 180

V. THE WORD INCARNATE OF JOHN 182

Chapter XV
SUMMARY AND CONCLUSION

I. FINAL ESTIMATE. *The cosmic Christ. Perfection of human character.* 187

II. PERSONAL POWER. *Leading traits. Teaching by contraries. The Messiah. (Davidic King, Son of Man, Suffering Servant.)* 189

III. SON OF GOD. *The Kyrios. Messianic title. The incarnate Logos.* 193

IV. CONCLUSION. 194

FOR FURTHER READING. 196

INDEX. 197

CHAPTER I

INTRODUCTORY

ANYONE who sets out to write a life of Jesus Christ must make clear from the beginning the terms under which he views his task. The very fact that he has used the double name for his hero shows at once that he does not seek to compose any ordinary biography. If the first name, Jesus, denotes the teacher of Nazareth, the second name, Christ, points to the belief that this Jesus was no ordinary man but the anointed of God, the Messiah. And that implies, even if it does not actually demand, some reference to the supernatural. Although the word Messiah was undoubtedly applied, at least on some occasions, to a purely human person, yet in this particular instance it is used to suggest that He who bore the title was a denizen of another world than this, and that His life in time and space can only be understood in the light of the eternal purposes of God.

Obviously if one believes that Jesus is the Christ in this sense the point of view is of such fundamental importance that it must colour all one's writing. In this respect we are in no better or worse plight today than those who compiled the first memoirs about Him. Many attempts have been made to disentangle the supernatural elements from the gospels and to reveal the residuum of a plain, unvarnished narrative of natural events. It was indeed a favourite occupation of the nineteenth-century liberals. The attempts, however, brought no general agreement and had to be abandoned. It is now quite clear that the evangelists wrote from a definitely theological point of view. They had no intention of stating objective facts without any sort of interpretation. The values they saw in their facts were spiritual and eternal. So closely indeed are fact and value interwoven in this narrative that it is quite impossible to eradicate theological bias from their record. If you eliminate the supernatural you are not left with a life of Jesus Christ as history has known Him but of someone quite different.

This does not mean that it is useless to try to be objective. Where facts are capable of being submitted to common historical judgment we must apply to them the same rigorous rules that we should use in writing secular history. But we must not be surprised if there are many apparent facts which do not submit themselves to that kind of judgment. That which belongs to a sphere outside space and time cannot be found within the categories of scientific knowledge. Nevertheless we must apply those categories wherever possible. If the results thus obtained receive a fuller meaning and a more ample explanation in the light of the supranatural claim, and especially if they can only be understood at all in the light of such a hypothesis, then we can be assured that that claim is as nearly reasonable as we can properly expect it to be. And if that claim fits into a consistent and rational interpretation of the universe as a whole, then we may feel justified in making the act of faith which enables us to accept it.

1. DID JESUS EXIST?

It may seem odd that the very existence of Jesus has been denied. By some humourless inquirers He has been reduced to a solar myth. By others He has been equated with the saviour gods who provided a rationale

INTRODUCTORY 3

for the 'mystery cults' that abounded in the Greco-Roman world. These fantasies may be safely regarded as curiosities of pseudo-historical investigation. Christianity has always claimed to be a historical religion. It has been prepared to stand or fall by the essential accuracy of its account of the events attendant upon its foundation. It has indeed its own documentary evidence, which we must examine in a moment. But there is also other evidence, which, if not strictly contemporary, is nevertheless early enough to possess great authority.

Suetonius (*c.* 65–140), in his *Life of Claudius* (xxv: 4), tells us that in the reign of that emperor (51 or 52?) the Jews were driven out of Rome for rioting *impulsore Chresto* 'at the instigation of Chrestus'. This is probably the pagan historian's effort to record the name of Christ, whom he regards apparently as still living in that year and as having been personally responsible for the outbreak. Its very inaccuracy lends an air of verisimilitude to the statement. The outbreak was probably the same disturbance that drove Aquila and Priscilla from Rome as recorded in Acts 18[2]. The truth of the matter no doubt is that disturbances had occured owing to Jewish opposition to Christians in the ghetto of Rome, and the police had impartially driven both parties out of the city. But at least Suetonius has no doubt of the existence of Christ. This conviction does not arise out of any favour for Christianity, for the same writer in his *Life of Nero* describes the Christians as 'a class of men given to a new and mischievous superstition'.

The way in which Nero attempted to foist the charge of the burning of Rome upon the Christians in A.D. 64 is described by Tacitus[1] (A.D. 54–119). He goes out of his way to explain how the hated sect arose. 'Christus,

[1] *Annals*, XV, 44.

from whom the name had its origin, suffered the supreme penalty during the reign of Tiberius at the hands of one of our procurators, Pontius Pilate.' That is clear evidence from the ablest historian of the Empire.

The younger Pliny, writing to Trajan about A.D. 112, tells what difficulties he is encountering as Governor of Bithynia in his efforts to eradicate the 'Christian superstition'. He notices how impossible it is to persuade true Christians to curse the name of Christ and describes their custom of meeting before daybreak to recite a hymn to Christ 'as though he were a god'.[1]

Good warrant is thus given in Roman literature for belief in the historical existence of Christ. This evidence can be reinforced from the side of Judaism. The text of Josephus (A.D. 37–100) as we now have it contains some long and interesting references to Jesus. But as the authenticity of these passages is in dispute they can hardly be taken as evidence. There is, however, one almost casual reference in the *Antiquities* (xx. ix: 81) written about A.D. 93–4 which establishes by inference the historical fact of Christ. 'Ananus assembled the sanhedrin of judges, and brought before them James, the brother of Jesus who was called Christ.' Among the Jews indeed there never was any doubt about the fact of Jesus' birth. Their anxiety to throw doubts upon its legitimacy is sufficient proof of that. Round about A.D. 85 the Rabbis were actually introducing a condemnation of Christians into their liturgy: 'May the Christians and heretics suddenly be laid low and not be inscribed with the righteous.'[2] It is hardly possible that an organisation could have developed with sufficient strength to demand

---

[1] Pliny, *Epp.* X, 96.
[2] Kilpatrick, *Origin of Gospel according to St. Matthew*, p. 109. O.U.P.

so formal a censure in so short a time on the basis of a mere legend without historical foundation.

II. CHRISTIAN SOURCES

This brings us to Christian sources. It might be urged that the best evidence for the historical fact of Christ is not to be found in literature but in the growth of the Church. It would be extremely difficult to find any credible reason for the sudden emergence of the Christian society except the factual existence of a founder. Christianity did not, like the mystery cults, look back to some ancient god. Its founder was a contemporary. The story of Jesus and His Church hangs together: it has all the appearance of verisimilitude; it purports to represent actual fact; from the outset it challenged denial and as far as the essential elements in the narrative go, never received it until our own times. The conclusion drawn by all but an occasional crank is that Jesus of Nazareth was a historical personage.

Of course if we admit the evidence of the Christian documents the question is put beyond dispute. Nor is there any reason why we should not admit their evidence. No literature in the world has been submitted to so careful a scrutiny. The searchlight of criticism that has played upon them for the last hundred years has shown them under a new aspect, but so far from discrediting them it has strengthened their credibility.

We now recognise St. Paul as the earliest of the New Testament writers. He was dictating his letters from A.D. 51 onwards, and so reveals knowledge of Jesus within twenty-two years of His Crucifixion. The only difficulty about St. Paul's evidence arises from his enigmatic saying about once knowing Christ in the flesh but now knowing Him so no more.¹ This has suggested to some ingenious minds that he was not interested in factual reality, but only in spiritual ideas. It is true of course that St. Paul often thinks of the cosmic Christ, of the Christ who was pre-existent before the world, who was God's agent in creation, who will come on the clouds of heaven to judge the world and who, having won final victory, will hand over His Kingdom to the Father. Colossians, Ephesians, Philippians are full of that kind of teaching. But St. Paul also knows about the crucifixion of Jesus: indeed he will take that as the sole subject of his preaching.² Also he knows that the cosmic Christ refused to cling to His equality with God and took on Himself the form of a slave.³ And he knows about the resurrection of Jesus, indeed more about the number of His appearances than any other contemporary writer.⁴ Thus the essential Christian doctrines are there, Incarnation, Atonement, Resurrection, and they are based upon what he regards as historical fact.⁵ All that Paul meant by not knowing Christ after the flesh was that the values of the Christ life were even more important than the historical details. There had been enough stating of the facts, he would now draw out their meaning. He was in the same position as the modern preacher, who says that he will no longer preach a dead but a living Christ.

The same kind of difficulty has been felt with regard to the Fourth Gospel. This is much the latest of the four gospels and is generally dated about the end of the first century. It is its difference from the other three gospels that earned the others the name of Synoptics, because they looked at their subject from a common point of

[1] 2 Cor. 5, 16.   [2] 1 Cor. 2^2.   [3] Phil. 2^6.   [4] 1 Cor. 15^{5-8}.
[5] For other details see Gal. 1^{19}, 4^4, Rom. 1^3, 9^5, 15^8, 1 Cor. 9^5.

INTRODUCTORY 7

view. St. John is unlike them since he appears less interested in the life of Jesus of Nazareth than in that of the eternal Son of God. He opens his gospel with a prologue giving quite clearly the point of view from which he is writing: 'In the beginning was the Word, and the Word was with God and the Word was God.' He goes on to show how this Word became incarnate and dwelt among men but was not recognised by the people to whom He came. The whole of the rest of the book is the working out in detail of this theme. It would, however, be a mistake to suppose that St. John was not interested at all in the factual events of Christ's life. On the contrary, they were quite necessary to his thesis. He was fighting on two fronts, trying to ward off the attacks of those who had begun to teach that Christ was a mere phantom and at the same time defending Him from the charge of being a mere creature of flesh and blood. Therefore he had to assert the facts—and that he does with meticulous care; and also to set them in their right relation to eternal reality—and that he does with such effect as to have earned for his book the title of 'the spiritual gospel'. Actually his book is the most interpretative of the gospels, but there can be no interpretation without facts, and the facts are there. Otherwise he could never have maintained his teaching of the flesh-and-blood reality of Christ.

The synoptic gospels seem much simpler. They are in many respects closely alike. They are of an earlier date. As they stand now, St. Matthew is generally put at about A.D. 85, St. Luke at A.D. 80, and St. Mark at A.D. 60.[1] They also display the same interests. They

[1] Nevertheless, when we refer to the First, Second, Third Evangelist, the reference is not to priority in time but to the order of the Gospels in A.V.

keep their feet much more firmly on the ground than St. John. That does not mean that there is no theological interpretation. There is, and it has been found very like that of St. John. But whereas St. John begins deliberately from the eternal, the synoptists begin from time—whether by way of a genealogical tree or by way of the preparatory mission of John the Baptist. The synoptics are also alike in that they share in common much of the same material. That fact has given rise to a quite fascinating literary problem. What are the mutual relations between these three books?

The old view was that Mark was an abbreviation of Matthew and Luke. The modern view is that Mark is the original from which Matthew and Luke drew much of their material. Of course Mark could not have been their only source. While Matthew appears to borrow from Mark about 590 verses and Luke 330, there are roughly 200 verses common to Matthew and Luke which are not to be found in Mark at all. The recognition of this fact led to the theory that there was a second source used by the first and third evangelists. To it is generally given the symbol Q, from the German *Quelle*, a source. This is what we know as the Two-Document Hypothesis.

Later, however, it was recognised that this theory did not give sufficient weight to the fact that there still remained a considerable amount of material that was not to be found in either Mark or Q but was peculiar to either Matthew or Luke. While Matthew has only about 190 verses of such material peculiar to himself, Luke has no less than 620. Obviously a theory that does not account for more than half of one of the gospels could not be regarded as entirely satisfactory. The way was thus opened for a Four-Document Hypothesis. The first and third evangelists are now credited with the possession each of a separate source of his own (M and L) in addition to Mark and Q. It is admitted that some of the material might come from local tradition but it is believed that the greater part of it was already written before it was used by the evangelists.

That carried the documentary analysis of the gospels as far as it could go.[1] But the work of analysis was by no means finished yet. If the gospels had thus been divided into their component documents, what lay behind the documents themselves? It was noted that the stories and incidents narrated in the documents tended to fall into stereotyped forms. Thus accounts of miracles follow a natural order—disease, cure, result. Short but pregnant sayings of Jesus (e.g. 'I came not to call the righteous but sinners') are prefaced by a statement of the circumstances that gave rise to the utterance. Longer sayings of our Lord take on the form of a brief sermon or exhortation. Stories about Jesus, apart from the Passion narrative, are easily separable from each other and fall into self-contained units such as the Baptism, Temptation, Transfiguration, the Woman taken in Adultery.

The conclusion leaps to the mind that we have here the original elements of the gospel story. Each of these comparatively small fragments could have been repeated orally by a preacher or a teacher many times. It is indeed the characteristic method of teaching in the East to reiterate a story or a short lesson until it is learnt by heart. In such a way these fragmentary portions may have been gone over so many times that they became stereotyped before they were committed to writing.

It is indeed a fine result of modern scholarship that at

[1] For a full account see Canon Streeter's great book *The Four Gospels*. Macmillan 1924.

last it puts us among the congregation at a primitive Christian sermon or among the learners imbibing their first knowledge of the details of the life and teaching of Christ from some venerated disciple or apostolic man. It bridges for us the gulf that has hitherto yawned between A.D. 30 and 50, between the end of the Lord's earthly life and the writing of these first documents which were later to be compiled into our synoptic gospels.

However, this 'form-criticism', as it is called, sets a new problem for the person who would write a life of Christ. A biography implies an orderly setting out of the facts. It demands that events should be narrated in chronological sequence. If, however, the gospels are fundamentally collections of fragments, how are we to be sure that the separate pieces have been arranged in order of date? It is possible that some quite different order has been imposed upon the incoherent mass of stereotyped oral traditions. Indeed the present tendency of scholarly research seems to lead towards the conclusion that the arrangement was dictated by liturgical needs. It is suggested that the material contained in the gospels was first read during the services, as 'lessons' are read today. This custom may have been responsible for the way in which the fragments have been grouped together.

The way in which this might be done can be seen most clearly in the Fourth Gospel, if at least one theory of its structure is correct. The basis of the arrangement would be the four festivals of the Jewish year. Lections, giving a Christian turn to the characteristic theme of each festival, would include a miracle narrative and an appropriate discourse. Thus the Passover (unleavened bread) is marked by the miracle of the multiplied loaves and the discourse on the Bread of Life (chs. 2–4 and 6). Pentecost

INTRODUCTORY 11

with its memorial of the publication of the Law, attracts the miracle at Bethesda and the discourse on Sabbath observance (ch. 5). The Feast of Tabernacles, at which there were ceremonies with water and the Temple candelabra, is associated with the healing of the blind man at the pool of Siloam and the discourse, 'If any man thirst' and 'I am the Light of the World' (chs. 7-9). Finally the Feast of Dedication with its commemoration of departed heroes recalls the raising of Lazarus and the discourse, 'I am the resurrection and the life' (chs. 10-11).[1]

As far as the synoptics are concerned, the Archbishop of Quebec has developed an even more thorough-going analysis of St. Mark's Gospel. Beginning with the theory that certain episodes might have been associated with stages in the agricultural and ritual year he found that the natural divisions of the gospel provided the requisite number of lessons. Proceeding further he found that the chapter enumeration in the oldest manuscript linked these arrangements with the Christian calendar. Finally he came to the conclusion that the gospel consists of a series of lections for the successive Sundays of the year.[2] Kilpatrick finds a similar motive at work in the composition of Matthew. He believes that Mark was not found to be an ideal book for lectionary use, and that Matthew compiled his gospel with the definite purpose of improving upon it.[3] The same method of analysis has not, so far as I know, been applied to the Third Gospel. It may indeed be rendered superfluous by St. Luke's introduction in which he says that his intention is to write 'in order', by

[1] Wand, *First Century Christianity*. O.U.P. 1937, pp. 128-9.
[2] Carrington, *A Primitive Christian Calendar*, Vol. I. O.U.P. 1951.
[3] Kilpatrick, *Origins of the Gospel according to St. Matthew*. O.U.P. 1946. (See especially Ch. IV.)

which he probably means chronological order. But St. Luke's sources were perhaps entirely written sources, and the documents with which he had to deal may have already been subjected to the necessities of liturgical arrangement.

The upshot of all this is that the would-be writer of a life of Christ has no guarantee that he can establish any chronological order in the events he has to relate. Of course that is only true within certain limits. Obviously the Birth narratives must come first and the Passion narrative, which was probably the earliest part of the story to be reduced to a coherent whole, must come last. But there is no certainty about the order of events between the Baptism and the week of the Passion, that is to say for the period of Jesus' ministry. Whether we can discern any general lines of development within this period remains to be seen.

III. FURTHER ESTIMATE

Such then are the main sources to which we must look for our information. The gospels are books of an unusual character and it is still not quite clear what purpose they were originally intended to serve. They are certainly not biographies in the usual sense. If Luke approximates most nearly to our modern notion of historical writing, the others are perhaps best regarded as memoirs designed to provide lections for reading in religious services. The documents of which they are composed may have served the purpose of handbooks to supplement the early sub-apostolic preaching and teaching. Even Mark may have been designed not only for public reading but also to put into permanent form a record of incidents in the Lord's ministry to which

INTRODUCTORY 13

a missionary could constantly refer. In the same way Q would provide an anthology of the Lord's utterances.[1]

In any case their true nature is revealed in the name by which in due course they came to be known. They are 'gospels', announcements of the 'good news' of the salvation wrought by Jesus Christ. They make known the historical incidents in which God was revealed through Christ and by which the way was made open for a complete reconciliation between God and man. They detail the points at which the horizontal line of space and time was struck by the vertical line of eternity. This did not mean that there was no abiding significance in other events but that here in a crucial period of history earth and heaven met. They thus constituted a challenge to the faith and allegiance of every reader.

This estimate of the character of the gospels is borne out by the references to Christ in other parts of the New Testament. They are generally speaking efforts to elucidate His teaching and draw out its consequences. They do not add much to our knowledge of the historical facts except in such an isolated instance as St. Paul's quotation of an otherwise unknown saying of Christ: 'It is better to give than to receive.'[2]

The apocryphal gospels on the other hand attempt to satisfy a not unnatural curiosity about further possible information on the Lord's life. Such books, however, can hardly be regarded as worthy of credence. They were generally written to bolster up some unorthodox view of our Lord's person and they originated at too late

[1] A few years ago much doubt was being expressed about the whole theory of Q. But the theory has gained much strength from the recent discovery of the Gospel of Thomas, a second century document of Gnostic provenance which consists entirely of (alleged) sayings of Jesus.
[2] Acts, 20^35.

a date for their evidence to be accounted trustworthy. Their tendency is to over-emphasise the mystical, not to say magical, elements they profess to recall from the unwritten records and memories of Jesus. To that extent they do at least reinforce belief in the suprahuman aspect of his life.[1]

All this brings us back to the point from which we started, namely that it is impossible to write the life of Jesus Christ as if it were that of a purely human person. Human, yes, but it is a humanity that has been assumed by the eternal Word of God and used as a means for making known the character of the Godhead in human terms. Many attempts have been made, particularly in Victorian times, to describe Jesus as an inspired prophet bringing to bear upon human affairs an insight and a wisdom that were unique in history. Much good work was done along these lines, and perhaps Seely's *Ecce Homo*[2] may be regarded as the finest example of the type. But the whole Liberal Protestant method of interpretation was countered by A. Schweitzer's *Quest of the Historical Jesus*. This investigation showed that, so far from Christ being depicted in the gospels as a calm, majestic figure laying down laws for an ethical governance of the world, there was at least as much evidence for regarding Him as a fervent Apocalyptist expecting the immediate end of the world and endeavouring in the short interval that remained to lift His followers into an absolute condition of morality bearing little relation to the needs of space and time. This flat contradiction to the commonplace interpretation of Jesus has led to a new and much more careful examination of the documents.

---

[1] They can be studied in M. R. James, *The Apocryphal New Testament*. O.U.P. 1924.
[2] Fifth Edition. Macmillan 1866.

It is now generally agreed that it is impossible to eliminate either the natural or the supernatural elements from the gospels even when they are reduced to their earliest origins in oral discourse. The facts as narrated are all shot through with theological implications. The obvious conclusion is that this was after all necessary because it was true to the historical situation. People spoke and wrote of Jesus in this way because they felt Him to be more than mere man. They faithfully described what they heard and saw. No doubt the tradition was moulded by later reflection. But it retained its primitive character. Jesus was both Son of Man and Son of God. It is from that point of view that we must still write of Him today.

IV. A NEW DIFFICULTY

A still further difficulty has been created for anyone who tries to write a life of Christ by the assertion of Professor Bultmann that the story as it at present exists partakes to a large extent of the nature of 'myth'. He claims that before one can get to the heart of the Christian message one must begin by 'demythologising' the gospels. The effect of this effort on his own method is shown in the first volume of his *Theology of the New Testament*, in which out of 350 pages in the English edition he devoted no more than thirty to the message of Jesus. As this has stirred up a considerable controversy we must devote some paragraphs to it.

The fundamental difficulty is to arrive at a satisfactory meaning of the term 'myth'. In Greek it meant originally anything uttered by word of mouth. It then came to mean a tale or a legend without regard to its truth or falsehood, and it was particularly applied to stories about gods and heroes. Gradually, however, the sense of fiction came uppermost and myth was contrasted with factual history. Consequently it is often used today as the precise contradictory of literal truth. As employed by scholars, however, it still retains something of its earlier indefinite colour. A modern dictionary defines it as a 'primitive tale imaginatively describing or accounting for natural phenomena especially by personification'. It may thus imply 'truth embodied in a tale', for the natural phenomena are there even if the tale is imagination. Myth often shades off into legend, and the recent tendency of historical research has been to discover a substratum of fact even in those ancient legends which were once dismissed as pure fiction. Archaeological discovery has thus for instance rehabilitated to a large extent many of the Homeric legends.

Theologians appear to be settling down to accept the definition of myth as 'the presentation of the unworldly and divine in terms of the worldly and human'. If we accept that definition we are compelled to ask in what other terms we could express the unworldly and divine. Those who believe in the Incarnation recognise in the earthly life of Jesus a revelation of the divine. The historical actuality of the life is a necessary element in the revelation: it could have been made in no other way. This does not mean that we need exclude the possibility of pictorial or poetic writing in the record. If we try to interpret literally the account of heavenly worship given in the Apocalypse we are reduced to the absurdity of material harps and golden crowns in the spiritual sphere. But if we accept the picture for what it manifestly is, a glowing description of adoration based on the customary worship of the Church on earth, we shall recognise its intrinsic truth.

That a distinction must sometimes be drawn between

truth and the manner of its expression is clear enough. But how far is the disintegration to go? It would be absurd to say that there is no such relationship as that of Father and Son in the Godhead because there is no physical generation in Heaven. Because we can give no physical explanation of the appearance of the angel Gabriel to Mary or of Satan to Jesus, are we to say that there was no Annunciation and no Temptation? It would seem far more scientific to lay hold of the essential reality of what occurred and then to try to understand as well as we can how it came to be expressed by our records in these particular terms. We may even come to the conclusion that after two thousand years we can find no better way of narrating the event than that given in the Scriptures.

If we depart so far from the principle of Incarnation as to divorce spiritual truth from its historical expression we shall be deserting the field of revealed religion for that of a Christian philosophy. Bultmann is aware of this danger, but believes that he escapes it by pinning his teaching fast to the existential Christ. But the distillation of quintessential truth as practised by this scholar has gone so far that there is extraordinarily little left of Jesus of Nazareth, and, as we have seen, Bultmann has little to say of Him. There must surely be a broader foundation for the immense edifice that Bultmann himself erects than the pinhead which is all that remains of his life of Christ.

It is probable that the whole controversy about 'demythologising' will die down as quickly as it has sprung up. It cannot subsist on its own terms for the very criterion of myth is to a large extent subjective. If it is impossible to say what is myth and what is not, it is obviously impossible to say how much of it there is in the New Testament. In effect the question raised is only another aspect of the age-long discussion about the supernatural element in the gospels. With that we deal at sufficient length elsewhere, and in so far as it relates to the miracles we devote to it a special chapter.

The method we have followed here is to let the documents speak for themselves, pointing out to what extent they support each other, while remembering that they are composed of 'forms' based upon an original oral tradition. It is becoming the custom of experts to go beyond even this dating and when they quote a particular passage to point out the reasons why they believe it to belong to the oldest or to a later strand in the tradition. We have not attempted this, both because the method is bound to be in large measure subjective and also because it would hold up the narrative and make far heavier reading than this small volume is intended to involve. We hope that enough has been said to show that we can still form a good historical picture of the life and character of Jesus and to point the way to further study on scientific and devotional lines. It is the conviction of the present writer that the core of the gospel story and our knowledge of the message of Jesus remain as sound as ever they were.

CHAPTER II

EARLY YEARS

1. PRELIMINARIES

WE have already realised that if we come to the New Testament for what we should nowadays regard as scientific history we are likely to be disappointed. The evangelists, no less than the other writers, are interested not so much in history as in the scheme of salvation. This does not mean, of course, that the plan of salvation has nothing to do with history. On the contrary, the two are indissolubly bound together. The gospels do not ignore history, but they are only interested in it in so far as it illustrates and reveals God's method of redemption. Consequently, while they are at considerable pains to expound and prove the way of God with man, they are content to state and take for granted what they believe to be historical facts. They are not equipped with a body of footnotes giving references to original sources.

The only kind of documentary 'proof' of which they make extended use is one peculiarly characteristic of the period. They endeavour to show that what happened in the life of Christ was completely consonant with God's age-old plan of salvation. What God intended to do had been shown to His people in the pages of the Jewish Scriptures. It was important therefore to show that the events of the life of Christ 'fulfilled' the prophecies of the Old Testament. This was true not only of His life as a whole but also of many details. We have only to remember the use made of such phrases as 'Out of Egypt have I called my Son'[1] and 'Not a bone of Him shall be broken'[2] to realise how anxious were the evangelists to show that Jesus was indeed the long promised Messiah. Today a great deal of attention is being given to this aspect of New Testament study and the questions of typology and symbolism form a large element in what is called 'Biblical Theology'.[3]

Obviously the scheme of salvation and the facts of history become most definitely involved with each other in the life of Christ. It is then, as we have already suggested, that heaven and earth most clearly met. Of that the evangelists are fully aware. All are concerned to show the importance of the moment. But each does it in his own way. Mark is content to relate how Jesus in His public ministry had a forerunner, a finger pointing like a sign-post to the Man-who-was-to-come. John carries the consideration to the courts of heaven. The eternal Logos, who had been with the Father 'in the beginning', was at this point of time made man. Matthew and Luke on the other hand adopt the biographical method of tracing the genealogical descent of Jesus. The former shows Him to have been the central figure of Jewish history, the latter reveals Him as the central figure in the history of the whole human race.

To start with a pedigree seems almost up to date. We are accustomed in modern biography to begin the story of a life by giving some account of our hero's ancestry. We feel that we know a man better if we have some knowledge of the stock from which he has sprung. We even think that in the long line of his forebears we may find some explanation of the particular combination of characteristic traits that make up his own special

[1] Mt. 2^{15}. [2] Jn. 19^{36}.
[3] See especially Austin Farrer, *St. Mark*. Dacre Press.

EARLY YEARS

genius. That, however, is hardly the intention of the first and third evangelists.

Matthew, writing for Jews, wishes to make clear to them that Jesus is their long expected Messiah. He therefore traces His legal descent from Abraham, the forefather of the race, through David to Joseph. No one would have been accepted as the Messiah who could not prove that he was a true Jew, and that he belonged to the line of the great King. It was customary among Oriental peoples to set great store by their pedigree. There are several instances in the Old Testament of the care with which this custom was observed in the case of priests and kings. One of the great reproaches against Herod the Great was that he could not fulfil this requirement. It would not have done for Christian apologists to allow Jesus to suffer from the same disability. There was indeed a Rabbinic saying, 'God lets His Shechinah dwell only in families that can prove their pedigrees.'

St. Luke has the further aim of showing Jesus' kinship to the whole human race. He therefore traces His descent back beyond Abraham to Adam, the first member of the race, who was himself 'the son of God'. As Luke was writing primarily for Gentiles it was important for him not to confine the genealogical interest to the Jews.

It is clear that the two trees are a mixture of history and symbolism, and it does not surprise us that there are differences between them. Matthew adheres to the straight royal line. Luke follows a side line through David's son Nathan, and also avoids Jehoiakim, who had been pronounced cursed by Jeremiah. Both, however, make clear the relation to David.

Another point in which they agree is that they trace the genealogy, not through Mary, the undoubted Mother of

Jesus, but through Joseph, His reputed father. This is no doubt due to the fact that legal descent was reckoned by the father's, not by the mother's, side; and that would be so, whether the father was true or putative. But it does raise the question in this case, whether Jesus had, or had not, a human father. It is to be noticed that both the first and third evangelists carefully refrain from describing Jesus as 'the son of Joseph'. Indeed Luke, who uses the phrase, deliberately inserts 'as was supposed', thereby suggesting its falsity.[1]

There can, of course, be no doubt that Christians already at this period believed in the Virgin Birth. Such a belief is implied in the story of the Annunciation[2] and in the angel's announcement to Joseph[3] in which the prophecy is quoted, 'Behold, the virgin shall be with child, and shall bring forth a son, and they shall call his name Immanuel' (Isa. 7^{14}). It is clear to the reader that already Christians interpreted this prophecy as they have done ever since, and saw it fulfilled in the miraculous Birth of Christ. It is equally clear to scholars that, as used in the original prophecy, the word translated 'virgin' was a somewhat vague term, which might have been applied to any young, unmarried woman, whether strictly virgin or not. It has therefore been suggested that an unwarrantably strict translation has been the *fons et origo* of the whole doctrine of the Virgin Birth, the story having been invented to fulfil the supposed prophecy. This, however, appears altogether too simple. The fact is that the poverty-stricken circumstances of the birth would in any case be little likely to commend the claim to Messiahship and the quotation from the Old Testament was eagerly seized upon to show that, after all, this humble appearance was in line with

[1] Lk. 3^{23}.   [2] Lk. 1^{34}.   [3] Mt. 1^{23}.

the purposes of God. It was not the quotation which explained the theory of the birth, but the birth itself which gave point to the quotation.

There are other circumstances attendant upon the birth, such as the glory-song of the angels, and the visit of the Magi, to say nothing of the strange incidents surrounding the birth of the forerunner, which suggest that the entry of Jesus into this life was not altogether natural. We cannot, however, use them as decisive arguments for a miraculous birth, because they are themselves among the least well attested events in the gospel narrative. They appear to have the support of only one or the other of two sources, and these sources are more steeped in wonders than the rest of the New Testament Scriptures. They are not sufficient in themselves to guarantee the historical truth of a supernatural generation.

In point of fact, however, no documentary evidence would be sufficient for such a purpose. No miracle can be proved by a purely historical argument. If we are in the end prepared to accept it, it will be because we are convinced of its truth on other grounds. All we can ask of the historical evidence is that it should be consonant with such other evidence as we have. While we should not be prepared to accept a supernatural event as true in the teeth of the historical evidence, we shall be ready enough to do so if we have other strong grounds for believing it, and find that the historical evidence, so far from refuting it, actually supports it.

That much at least we can in the present case affirm. To get absolutely reliable evidence would be, in a matter of so intimate a nature, in any case impossible. We have only to remember the great perplexity that surrounds the stories of many births in royal families to know how difficult is the historian's task in such instances. In the present case many scholars have believed that they can trace the details given by Matthew back to Joseph, while others have been equally sure that the account in Luke must have come from Mary. All agree that there would inevitably have been considerable reticence about the mystery in the earliest years. To narrate it formed no part of the plan of the second and fourth evangelists. St. Paul says nothing that would make it appear unlikely. We are fortunate to have so early an attestation of it as appears in Matthew and Luke.

The Virgin Birth is accepted because it appears consonant with the dignity of an Incarnation. It fits in with the whole scheme of redemption. It agrees as well with the entry of the Son of God upon this earthly scene as the Resurrection and Ascension agree with His exit from it. It harmonises, as well as we are able to judge, with the whole plan of salvation. That is no doubt why it was accepted as true by the early generations of Christian believers. That is why we can still accept it today.

II. THE NATIVITY

St. Luke, who adopts more nearly than any other New Testament writer the method of the modern historian, tries to pin down for his readers the exact date and circumstances of the birth. He tells us that it took place during the reign of the Emperor Augustus on the occasion of a general census. Nothing, however, is known of a universal census under Augustus. It is possible, of course, that St. Luke has given prominence to a census that was only local and partial. Colour is lent to the suggestion by his further statement that the census was first taken when the Governor of Syria was a

EARLY YEARS

certain Quirinius. This, sad to say, does not help us very much, as Quirinius did not become governor or legate until A.D. 6, which is too late a date for the birth of Jesus. We know, however, on the testimony of Josephus that Quirinius did hold an 'enrolment'. Such a step would be possible at that time because Archelaus had been deposed and Palestine had come under direct Roman government. Some scholars, however, believe they have discovered evidence that Quirinius was Governor of Syria for two periods and that the earlier was about B.C. 10–7. But those are the dates generally accepted for Saturninus, under whom as Tertullian tells us there was a census.[1] It is possible that Luke has confused the names, but B.C. 7 is probably too early a date for the Birth of Christ. Luke (1^5) tells us that He was born when Herod was king, and as Herod the Great died in B.C. 4 it is usual to take that as the most likely date of Jesus' birth.

We must conclude that it is impossible in the present state of our knowledge to elucidate precisely the historical details surrounding the Birth of Christ. In that respect, of course, His birth is subject to the same obscurity that shrouds the birth of all the heroes of antiquity. If in this one single instance everything had been exactly recorded beyond the possiblity of cavil we might have become somewhat suspicious. It seems only natural that the evangelists, writing in the true character of their time, should be less careful of historical exactitude than of the spiritual and moral beauty of their story. That they have given us a poem of incomparable loveliness no one will deny. But it belongs to the type of poetry that derives its highest value from the factual truth of the main event

---

[1] In any case the theory of two periods of governorship for Quirinius has not been confirmed by recent scholarship.

it portrays. That Jesus *was* born, and in the circumstances of the census disclosed by the gospel narrative, admits of no real dispute. What can we say of the other incidents recorded as associated with His birth?

That the entrance of the Son of God into the conditions of human life should be accompanied by unusual portents would be naturally expected by any writer of imagination. The surprising thing is that our authorities record so little that is not capable of commonplace explanation. It is in keeping with the whole observable plan of revelation, that God will not force belief in Himself: there must always be room for variety of interpretation, and consequently for the exercise of faith on the part of the believer.

The birth of Jesus took place in the midst of the humblest, and indeed the most humiliating circumstances. He was born in no royal household, but in the family of a small craftsman. Joseph, who had been reassured by a vision as to his bride's chastity and had refused to disown her, could find no better place for the delivery of her child than a stable in the crowded village of Bethlehem, to which they had been driven by the necessity of the census. It was as if the Eternal Word, having decided to enter the world of men, deliberately chose to become man at the lowest level of human comfort. True, there were lower grades of civilisation and culture than were to be found in Palestine, but if the revelation were to be adequately made, a point must be chosen where it could be understood. As we shall see, Joseph and Mary, however lowly their condition, nevertheless shared in the high religious and cultural training of their race. To people of such refinement the surroundings of the stable would be even more trying than to others of coarser upbringing.

Beyond Joseph and Mary it was only a group of shepherds in the immediate neighbourhood who appear to have been aware that anything unusual had occurred. The lovely story of the visions of angels and their celestial music comes to us on the unsupported evidence of Luke's individual source. Many ingenious explanations of its origin have been suggested in the association of pagan hero-myths with shepherds, or alternatively with the presence on these hills in ancient times of David, the Jewish shepherd-king. None of them has won general acceptance, and it seems easier to believe that there is a genuine historic foundation for the story. To what extent it received embellishment in the light of later understanding of the sacred birth, it is perhaps idle to inquire.

If the first 'sign' was thus given to humble shepherds, Matthew's special source tells us that another was given to a very different class of people—the Magi of Persia. They were professional astrologers, whose aid was much sought in attempts to forecast the future, and they often achieved considerable standing in the court and society. They are said to have been stirred by some astronomic phenomenon to believe that a person destined to become King of the Jews had been born in Jerusalem. When they found that there was no new birth at the palace of Herod they were led to Bethlehem, where they found the Child and offered the gifts they had brought.

Again ingenious attempts have been made to identify the occurrences that started the Magi on their journey. Some have found it in the conjunction of Jupiter and Saturn in Pisces, some in the appearance of the dog-star Sirius at sunrise. If we could identify the star it might give us precise indications of the date of the Saviour's birth. Such efforts, however, are misplaced. We have no means of knowing what celestial phenomena would indicate to Persian astrologers a royal birth. The fact that they would have sufficient faith in their own professional skill to act upon such indications is inherently probable. We can enjoy the picturesqueness of the narrative and admire the quality of their devotion even if we cannot identify the star they saw. And above all we may reflect upon the divinity of the means by which God directs inquirers to Himself.

The picture, however, has its sinister side. The inquiries had aroused the jealousy of Herod, and when he could obtain from the Magi no precise information as to the identity of the new-born pretender, he sought the safety of his dynasty by putting to death the infant children of the village. There is, of course, no precise verification of this massacre, which in any case would not involve a great number of deaths, but it is in complete accord with the known character of Herod the Great. One of his last acts was to procure the murder of his eldest son, and Josephus even goes so far as to say that he ensured general mourning at the time of his own death by ordering that one member out of each family of his subjects should be slain.

Warned in time of Herod's evil intentions, Joseph escaped with the Child and His mother into Egypt. There the family remained until the death of the king. Then they returned, not to Bethlehem, but to the Galilean town of Nazareth, where Joseph had formerly lived and worked. Matthew sees in these journeys an epitome of the former wanderings of Israel, which would be particularly appropriate for one who was to be their Messiah, and he quotes in reference to them the words of Hosea, 'Out of Egypt have I called my Son.' This is

EARLY YEARS

in accordance with the common effort of the earliest Christian apologists to find parallels to the life of Christ in Old Testament history.[1]

III. NAZARETH

It was in Nazareth of Galilee that Jesus was brought up. We shall have a good deal to say in the next chapter about His environment. Here it will be sufficient to notice that His education was thoroughly religious. He had already, according to the usual custom, been circumcised when He was eight days old. Circumcision was the rite by which Jewish boys were admitted individually into the Covenant made between Jehovah and His chosen people. In accordance with its terms Jehovah had promised to make Israel a blessing to all the nations of the earth, and Israel on its part undertook to serve Jehovah faithfully and to foreswear all other gods. Any boy who reflected as he grew to manhood upon his part in this Covenant would obviously feel resting upon himself a very definite responsibility. For Jesus this sense would be heightened by the personal name that was then, as was customary, bestowed upon Him. Jesus, or Joshua, was an honoured name among the Hebrews, and meant 'Jehovah is our salvation.'

Mary was punctilious in the observance of her religious duties. Shortly after the Circumcision she went with her husband to Jerusalem and there in the Temple, the central shrine of Judaism, offered the usual thanksgiving for the birth of the Babe. The two were amazed when a pair of aged prophets, Simeon and Anna, hailed the Child as the long promised Messiah. Luke, who is fond of poetry, has recorded that the former gave

[1] See Dodd, *According to the Scriptures, passim.* Nisbet.

utterance to his ecstatic joy in the prophetic lyric which we know as the *Nunc Dimittis*.

Our knowledge of these two events, the Circumcision and the Purification, is derived from Luke's special source, but they have an obvious verisimilitude as belonging to the normal religious life of devout Jews. The salutation of the Child as Messiah is the more readily understood if we assume, as we are assuredly entitled to do, that Mary had confided to her cousin Elizabeth the unprecedented manner in which her Child had been conceived. While such a thing would not be allowed to become the subject of common gossip, some whisper of it may well have reached the ears of such semi-professional frequenters of the Temple as were already looking for 'the redemption of Israel'.

These events, of course, had preceded the flight into Egypt. They are mentioned here in order to emphasise the specially religious atmosphere that would pervade the home at Nazareth. They would inevitably surround the growing Boy with an even stronger sense of expectation than is common in any household where children are pursuing their normal development to maturity, and looking forward to their future work in the world.

Of Jesus' boyhood we have only one recorded incident. This occurred at the age of twelve, when His parents showed again their specially devout character by following their usual custom of travelling to Jerusalem for the Passover Feast. On that occasion Jesus joined the classes surrounding the teachers who were expounding the Law in the Temple courts. He amazed everyone by the intelligence with which He joined in the usual routine of question and answer, and had become Himself so engrossed that He failed to realise that the caravan to which His party belonged had started on the return

EARLY YEARS

journey. When His parents at last missed Him, and returned to find Him still eagerly attending the classes they were surprised at the boyish literalness with which He had interpreted the injunction to occupy oneself with spiritual affairs. 'Know ye not that I must be about My Father's business?' (or in My Father's house).[1]

This incident shows that Jesus enjoyed to the full the educational facilities of His people. The Jews were proud of their schooling. Inevitably the earliest knowledge would be imbibed from the mother, but the duty was actually laid upon the father to teach the son, and every other duty must give place to that. Naturally the learning was mainly religious, but it involved being able first to repeat, and later to read, the Scriptures. At the age of five or six every child went to school. The schools were held in the synagogues or in specially allotted buildings, and the teacher was generally the Chazzan or Officer of the synagogue. The children sat in a semicircle on the ground looking towards the teacher, who also sat on the floor.

For the first four years the Scriptures would be the only textbook. From ten to fifteen years of age the pupil would also study the 'tradition' which by the second century was incorporated in the Mishna. If he did not show particular aptitude this would be the end of his education, but if he displayed promise he would be allowed to go on to one of the academies established by the Rabbis, where he would hear much elaborate comment on the Scriptures. At least this was the system in vogue in later centuries, and there had probably been few changes. Together with the services in the synagogue, where of course the Scriptures were read and instructional discourses delivered, this would form a very thorough

[1] Lk. 2⁴⁹.

training in morals and character. It would also afford some training in the study of language, for the Scriptures were not written in the current, conversational Aramaic, but in the ancient, strictly classical Hebrew.[1]

[1] For a more adequate account of Jewish educational methods see Edersheim's *Life and Times of Jesus the Messiah*, I. 230 ff. But he is inclined to date the Mishna and Talmud much too early, and it is not clear how far the evidence of later times can be read back into the conditions of our Lord's time.

CHAPTER III

ENVIRONMENT

1. PALESTINE A PALIMPSEST

THE reference to Jesus' education leads inevitably to a discussion of His surroundings, for environment, whether physical or mental, is one of the most potent elements in the training of character. In this respect Jesus can be studied like other men. The nature in which the Logos became incarnate was that of man, not of mutilated man, but of complete man. The Word could not reveal the nature of God-head except through that of perfect, all-round manhood. We must therefore expect the life of Jesus to present most of the usual features of human biography. We must see what were likely to be the effects of His environment on His human mind.

Palestine, and particularly Galilee, was a point at which diverse races, languages and cultures met. For centuries it had served as a highway between the rival empires of Assyria and Egypt. It had been invaded from the coast and from the desert. Only when there had been a stalemate between the warring nations had it enjoyed leisure to develop a civilisation of its own. More often it had been expected to adopt that of one of its temporary masters. By the time of Christ it was at once a polyglot and a palimpsest. This explains the seeming paradox that the Jews clung to the purity of their ancestral culture more tenaciously than any other nation under heaven, and that, at the same time, one can never be sure how far outside elements have crept into it.

In dealing with the history of the early Christian Church one can generally make shift to distinguish between eastern and western traits. In the case of St. Paul one is always separating the Roman citizen from the Jewish Rabbi. Even in dealing with the contemporary Alexandrian philosopher, Philo, one strains out the diverse thought of Moses and Plato. But in the case of Jesus Christ the difficulty is far greater. He is a Jew certainly, thoroughly imbued with the knowledge of the Scriptures and the ancestral teaching. But there are fundamentally contrasting strains, and one is tempted to look for some of them in the classical background. Yet proof is hard to come by. It is far easier, for instance, to pick out national traits in the thought of Shakespeare than in that of Jesus of Nazareth, while sheer universalism is more obvious in the writings of Marcus Aurelius. Nevertheless, we must do our best to sketch the many-coloured background of the tapestry against which His own portrait stands out in such heroic proportions. We may begin with the border and work towards the centre.

The prevailing culture of the time was Greco-Roman. In the east the Greek element in it was Hellenistic. Ever since the conquests of Alexander in the fourth century B.C. there had gone on a close intermingling between the civilisations of Greece and the eastern nations. It is the resulting culture which is known by the epithet Hellenistic. The gymnasia and the delight in physical culture so characteristic of Greece were mingled with the cults and religions of the mysterious east. Philosophy was cultivated by the intellectual few, but the majority had learnt to think themselves fortunate if they belonged to a 'mystery cult'. This professed to link them with some god who represented in his own myth the death and rising again of nature, and so to give them freedom from the grip of fate (*heimarmene*) and to guarantee them a blissful immortality. One of the successors of Alexander, Antiochus Epiphanes, tried in the middle of the second century B.C. to force the Jews to relinquish their own law and to accept the Hellenistic culture in its place. Under the Maccabees the Jews put up an epic resistance and preserved for a time their integrity. Later, however, various elements in the nation began to make terms with pagan thought and customs. Even some of the 'wise men', the compilers of the wisdom literature, were willing to learn from the Greek philosophers. Such books as Wisdom and Ecclesiasticus betray the influences of this broadening of outlook, and it is not improbable that some knowledge of them reached the home of Jesus.

It would indeed have been impossible for the Jews to have escaped such influences altogether in view of the Dispersion (Diaspora). Great numbers of them lived in pagan towns and countries. There was a Jewish ghetto in every great city around the Mediterranean. The Jewish element was perhaps most important in Alexandria. There it had great influence in the university and there it produced the greatest contemporary philosopher, Philo. Still more important was the production of a Greek version of the Scriptures known to us as the Septuagint (LXX), which included, besides the limited canon of the Hebrew Old Testament, the section familiar to us as the Apocrypha. It is sometimes said that the Jews of the Dispersion were more meticulous in their observance of the Law than the residents of Jerusalem. Perhaps they tried to be, but their circumstances were such that they could not help themselves. In such close contiguity with the richness of the pagan world they must, even in spite of themselves, have imbibed something of its characteristic modes of thought. We are bound to learn even from those whom we most strongly oppose.

This amalgam of Greek and eastern elements was overlaid by Roman law and order. Pompey took Jerusalem in B.C. 63 and thereafter the Romans tried to organise Palestine as a buffer State against possible invasion of their empire from the east. They did not worry much about its religion or culture so long as nothing was allowed to interfere with its loyalty to Rome. They were even willing to leave it as far as possible its own native rulers. Herod the Great, who after all was not a native, but a hated Idumean, was allowed by Augustus to retain the throne after the battle of Actium in B.C. 31. He ruled till B.C. 4, marking his reign by the rebuilding of the Temple, as well as by appalling cruelties. Thereafter Antipas ruled in Galilee, and Philip on the other side of Jordan. Archelaus held Judea till A.D. 6, but then he was removed and a Roman Procurator, Pontius Pilate, was put in his place. Over the whole country, known to government administration as the province of Syria, was set the imperial legate, Quirinius.

II. JEWISH PARTIES

To their Roman governors the Judeans were always something of a problem. Their habitual turbulence made them unhappy partners on the fringe of empire. The Romans tried to sooth them by allowing them the full exercise of their religion and by refraining from demanding of them the usual recognition of the divinity of Rome and the Emperor. But even when their fierce nationalism did not unite them against their masters, they were likely to make trouble through their internal quarrels. Small as were their numbers, they were divided into several parties.

The Herodians, as the name implies, were a court party subservient both to the native ruler and the imperial power. The Sadducees were a much stronger body, including most of the hierarchy and the native officials. They stood for traditional religion and the strict letter of the Law. They would admit no new notions and were specially opposed to the doctrine of a future life. They held the majority on the Sanhedrin, that is the central council of seventy which acted as a sort of parliament for the Jewish people. They probably included among their number also most of the 'elders', that is the members who composed the Little Sanhedrin or council of each local synagogue. These synagogues might consist, not of what we should call parishioners, but groups of people with some special interest in common. Thus there might be a synagogue of freedmen, or later even of Jewish Christians.

The Pharisees were, from the religious point of view, the most important party. They are often coupled with the Scribes, that is the men who not only reduplicated copies of the law, but also commented upon it. The name 'Pharisees' itself probably connotes those who divided or analysed, and so interpreted, the text. In the course of their studies they extended the law to deal with special cases (*halaka*), much as a modern casuist applies the canon law, and they also illustrated it with comments and examples (*haggada*). They were descended from the specially pious section of the community (Hasidim) who had achieved especial fame in the Maccabean period. In the course of time they had developed a strong belief in the angelic world and in the resurrection. By our Lord's time they had suffered considerable deterioration and were often rebuked by Him for their hypocrisy.

The Zealots were a fanatically patriotic party. They were largely responsible for a number of risings against the Romans. In the dreadful siege of Jerusalem in A.D. 70 they degenerated into terrorists (Sicarii), who were as ready to butcher the moderates among their own compatriots as to turn their arms against the foreign soldiers. At an extreme remove from them were the Essenes, a small semi-monastic section who subjected themselves to certain forms of asceticism, rejoiced in religious services and sought escape from the world in hallowed seclusion.[1]

III. GEOGRAPHICAL DIVISIONS

Judea was not the whole of Palestine. Immediately to the north of it lay Samaria, an extensive district with a chief town of the same name. Its inhabitants were regarded by the Judeans as utterly without the pale. They were the descendants of the mixed race resulting from the forced migrations under the Assyrian conquests of the eighth century B.C. They practised, and a remnant of them still practise, a kind of bastard Judaism, which earned them the undying contempt of their southern neighbours.

[1] It is believed that the discovery of the Dead Sea Scrolls has thrown considerable light on the Essenes. The scrolls, found in a cave at Qumran near the Dead Sea, formed the library of a religious community with a carefully planned constitution and way of life. The community seems to have originated as a result of strained relations between an ardently pious group of Jews and Alexander Jannaeus (c. 103 B.C.) and to have lasted till the Roman advance against the Jewish rebels in A.D. 68. There is, however, no evidence that either John the Baptist or Jesus was ever in actual contact with them.

Farther north lay Galilee. Canon Streeter once said that Christianity was 'mostly a Galilean affair'. It is specially important that we should understand the conditions prevailing in the district where Jesus spent most of His time. A key to such understanding is offered in the phrase 'Galilee of the Gentiles'. From the point of view of the superior people in Jerusalem it was scarcely less heathen than Samaria. Its Jewish residents were within the Covenant, but they were subject to so many pagan influences that not much could be expected of them. 'Can any good thing come out of Nazareth?' 'Search and see that out of Galilee ariseth no prophet.' These New Testament references can be reinforced from the Rabbis: 'Galilee, Galilee, thou hatest the law, therefore thou shalt yet find employment among robbers' (J. ben Zaccai). Archaeological evidence shows how Jews in Galilee broke the strict Mosaic law by introducing human and animal figures in the decoration of their synagogues. The influence of the many Greco-Roman cities in the neighbourhood must have affected more than the architecture. Rabbinical scholars draw attention to the prevalence of demonology in Galilean thought.[1]

Another type of thought that has often been specially associated with Galilee is that of the Apocalyptists. They were the writers who succeeded to the great prophets in the centuries immediately preceding the birth of Christ. They are distinguished by the exuberance of their symbolic language and more particularly by their habit of foreshortening the future. They wrote at times when the condition of things appeared so bad that deliverance could only be expected if God put forth His own right hand and rescued His people by some great cataclysm.

[1] I have discussed the existence of Hellenistic influences in Galilee in my *Development of Sacramentalism*, pp. 72 ff. Methuen.

The most conspicuous example of this kind of literature in the Old Testament is the Book of Daniel; in the Apocrypha there is 2 Esdras, and in the New Testament the Revelation of St. John the Divine. Other examples are to be found outside the Canon. As we shall see later, there are evidences of this type of presentation in the teaching of Christ, and at least one important school of theologians thinks that this gives us the key to the interpretation of His whole mind.[1]

IV. JUDAISM

It would be a gross mistake if we thought that the picture presented by Judaism was wholly unattractive to contemporaries. Religion during the first century B.C. was at a low ebb. If there had ever been any life in the old pagan myths, they had long ceased to be much more than poetic fancies. The eastern faiths had degenerated by way of the mystery cults into theurgy and magic. The Caesar-worship of the Roman Empire was never more than a formal imposition of the State. Only philosophy remained to inculcate an austere morality. In contrast to all this the Jews stood out in the possession of their Scriptures, and in the majesty of their Law. They believed in one God only and they equated His character with moral goodness. Some of them even pledged reward or punishment to good and evil after death. There was nothing like this elsewhere. It enriched the best teaching of philosophy with the vital warmth of personal religion. It embodied its worship in a dignified cult of psalms and prayers, lessons and sermons. Only in the central shrine at Jerusalem was there a more ornate service with the accompaniment of animal sacrifice, and

[1] See above, p. 14, on Schweitzer.

that was so remote from most pagans as to acquire the mysterious enchantment of the half-known and barely understood. It was not strange that there should be many converts to Judaism from the Greco-Roman world.

The difficulty for converts was that, if they wished to accept Judaism wholly, they must disavow their race as well as their religion, and enter the Jewish nation and Church by the rite of circumcision. This was to ask more than all but a very few were willing to give. Most of those who were attracted by the nobility of Jewish faith and morals were content to become mere hangers-on of the synagogue. They could imbibe all the teaching and try to live the life, but without being fully committed and without forsaking their own people. Of such partial converts there was a considerable number. From the very first they proved particularly amenable to the influence of Jesus, and among them the Christian Church found many adherents. Christ offered freely privileges for which Moses demanded too severe a price. It is easy to understand the jealousy of the Jewish authorities.

The bridge between the proselyte and the synagogue or the Church, was most likely to be found in that section of society to which the family of Jesus belonged. What used to be called 'the special seed-plot of Christianity' was the 'Am-Ha' arez' or 'People of the Land'. Recently a good deal of doubt has been cast upon the identity of these folk and it is possible that they were not so clear-cut a section of society as once scholars thought them to be. But there are too many indications of a special type of person in association with Jesus to warrant the complete dismissal of the suggestion.

In the Old Testament the title 'People of the Land' is applied to the common people in distinction from whatever passed in those times for the nobility and gentry.

The hierarchy despised them because they 'knew not the law', and in New Testament times they were frequently dubbed accurst by the Pharisees for that reason. It is significant that they seem to have numbered among their ranks many 'publicans' (tax collectors) and 'sinners' (people who sat loose to the law). Some of the Rabbis at least associated them especially with Galilee; and that would chime in with the obvious fact that there were many people of the apocalyptist type in the entourage of Jesus. Mary may suggest a special trait of their character and even their rank in society, when in the *Magnificat* she speaks of the 'humble and meek'; and Simeon may reveal both their special interest in the coming of the Messiah and in the salvation of foreigners, when he speaks of the Babe who had come 'to be a Light to lighten the Gentiles' as well as to be the 'glory of God's people Israel'. Such a special group would not be confined to Galilee, but they were specially numerous there. In any case there does seem to be sufficient evidence that there was a simpler, broader outlook as well as a richer and tenderer aspiration among some of the shepherds, fishermen, tax gatherers and devotees who surrounded the holy family, than in the circles of official Judaism. It was in this special environment that Jesus grew to manhood.

CHAPTER IV

BEGINNING OF THE MINISTRY

1. JESUS AT HOME

HOW Jesus spent His youth and early manhood we have no means of knowing. It is generally assumed that He entered the trade of His putative father and became a carpenter. If, as is generally supposed, though without any means of verification, Joseph was an elderly man, it is quite possible that he died soon after Jesus attained adult manhood. In that case Jesus may have become an independent tradesman and the support of His mother. There is no indication that during this period He was at all interested in what one might call the higher education of the pagan towns, or that He ever became involved in any of the political movements of His own people. That He was intensely observant of the daily life of His neighbours and sensible of the natural beauties of the countryside we can deduce from the form in which much of His teaching was cast. On the whole one gains the impression of a quiet and religious youth who shared to the full the social life of His home town, pursuing His own business with steady industry, but avoiding the open stage of public affairs. As a boy He had 'increased in wisdom and stature and in favour with God and man'. The picture appears to remain valid even after His physical growth was complete. There can, of course, be no doubt that He meditated deeply upon the spiritual condition of His country. It is significant that the event which drew Him out of His retirement was a mission undertaken by His relative John, who, because of his special methods, became known as the Baptist. It is with an account of this mission that St. Mark opens his gospel.

John was the son of a priest, Zacharias, whose wife Elizabeth was also a member of a priestly family. There had been unusual circumstances connected with his birth which would naturally, as he came to know of them, give him the sense of a special vocation. He seems all his life to have practised a somewhat severe asceticism, and, in spite of his ecclesiastical connections, to have grown up with a feeling of profound dissatisfaction with the prevailing religious sentiment of his times. Unlike Jesus, he withdrew from ordinary social life and spent much of his time as a desert recluse. Even in such details as food and dress he reverted to the old prophetic type. Like the prophets he inveighed equally against excessive luxury, false religion and moral degeneracy.

Somewhere about A.D. 26, the fifteenth year of Tiberius, John appeared in Judea and inaugurated what may be regarded as the last of the great prophet reforms in Judaism. The two planks in his platform were a call to prepare for the immediate coming of the Messiah, and a demand for moral regeneration. He preached with the vehemence and the boldness of a Latimer. No class escaped the lash of his scorn, and each was told in the most practical fashion what they must do to give proof of their penitence. Those who were prepared to join him could do so by undergoing a rite of baptism in the waters of Jordan. The Jews were well accustomed to washings as a symbol of purity and renewal, but never had baptism assumed so great an importance as in this movement of John's. Hence the name of the Baptiser or Baptist by which he was commonly known. It implies that he

BEGINNING OF THE MINISTRY 45

himself performed the 'washing' and did not leave it, as was customary, to the individual.

Jesus could not remain aloof from this movement. All His thoughts and experience made Him realise that this was far the best thing in the contemporary world. His own sense of unique vocation may have been quickened by the thought of that Messiah whose approach the followers of the movement believed to be imminent. He must at least associate Himself with His kinsman and give him what moral support He could. He left the peaceful obscurity, to which He would never return, and repaired to Jordan, where John was baptising.

II. JESUS' BAPTISM

It is generally accepted that Jesus was now thirty years of age. St. Luke at least tells us that He was about thirty (3^{23}) and that agrees with the fact that He could not have been born later than B.C. 4, which is the probable date of the death of Herod the Great. This conclusion receives significance from the fact that thirty was the customary age at which a Jewish 'teacher' might enter upon his career. But there is no reason to believe, as some have done, that the dates have been manipulated to fit this custom.

Jesus' appearance among His hearers and His request for baptism seem to have occasioned John considerable surprise. No doubt the two were well acquainted, and John knew enough of Jesus' character to feel that he was not himself worthy to occupy the place of leader where Jesus was concerned, nor could he feel that Jesus had any need to share in a rite that was accompanied by repentance for sins committed. Jesus, however, insisted. This was the rite by which one entered into the whole movement with its double emphasis upon moral purity and preparation for the coming of the Messianic Kingdom. It would be proper for Him to share in it, so that He should be seen to be completely committed to the reformation of Israel. Thus He and John would both do what was fitting to 'fulfil all righteousness'.

However, John himself had realised that the significance of baptism could not be exhausted by the meaning he had himself attached to it. He had said that a greater than he would come and would baptise not only with water, but with Spirit and with fire. Jesus Himself experienced a fulfilment of this promise in His own case. As He came out of the water 'He saw the heavens rent asunder, and the Spirit as a dove descending upon Him: and a voice came out of the heavens, "Thou art My beloved Son, in Thee I am well pleased." [1] That is Mark's, the earliest, account and it is highly symbolic, written in Rabbinic terms. The old three-storied conception of the universe had been elaborated by the incorporation of many heavens, one above the other. Sometimes the curtain of these successive heavens was drawn aside. God, however, no longer appeared in person or in His 'Angel'. People could not even hear His voice direct. Occasionally, however, some favoured individual might be allowed to hear the Bath Qol—the daughter of the voice, the echo. This Bath Qol was often identified with the Spirit and both were represented under the symbol of a dove. The passage then is as vivid a form as a writer of the period could employ to assert that at that moment God spoke to the inner consciousness of Jesus with a clarity and certainty of the most vivid kind. It affirmed for Jesus all the sense of vocation with which He had grown up, and it reinforced His consciousness of unique relation to the Father.

[1] Mk. 1^{10-11}.

How much of this was known or suspected by John or any of his followers it is not easy to say. The Fourth Gospel, assuming its interpretative role thus early in the narrative, omits the account of the baptism, which was already well known, and substitutes for it an interview with a deputation of Priests and Levites, in which John explains that he is not himself the Messiah, but is preparing the way for Messiah's coming.[1] Next day John actually identifies Jesus as the Lamb of God, and declares how he has seen the Spirit in the form of a dove resting upon him.[2] Jesus is thus proclaimed from the outset as the future Saviour, who will take away the sin of the world and will baptise, not with water merely, but with the Holy Spirit. If this is factual history, and not a reading back into the beginning of something that only became clear much later, we must still recognise that at the time only a few were admitted into the secret or were able to grasp it. It was His own urgent need to understand it and to work out its consequences, that drove Jesus straightway to seek solitude in the wilderness.

III. THE TEMPTATION

The experience that followed is generally known as the Temptation. We are able to judge its character by the vivid, but highly symbolic picture presented by the synoptists. Mark mentions the incident, but most of the details are from Q, whose story is repeated with unimportant variations by both Matthew and Luke.[3] What happened came as the culmination of a prolonged fast of forty days. It is represented as an encounter between Jesus, under the fresh impetus of the Spirit, and the demonic adversary of God and man. We are left to

[1] Jn. $1^{19\text{ff}}$. [2] Jn. $1^{29\text{ff}}$. [3] Mk. 1^{12-13}, Mt. $4^{1\text{ff}}$, Lk. $4^{1\text{ff}}$.

suppose that it had now become clear to Jesus that He must undertake Messiah's mission. The question with which He is wrestling is that of the proper method by which the task shall be pursued. The devil suggests several ways in which the work can be expedited by making concessions to the spirit of this world.

The first temptation is to spare Himself physical hardship by using the special powers of which He might feel Himself possessed as 'Son of God'. After the long fast He naturally felt the pangs of hunger. A few stones may have suggested by their shape the round *chapatties* or loaves of the east. Why not turn them into actual bread and so spare Himself unnecessary inconvenience? But He would not use His powers for selfish ends or on so low a level. There was something far more important than physical hunger. Spiritual gifts must be used for spiritual purposes. 'Man does not live by bread alone, but by every word that proceeds from the mouth of God.' It was spiritual, not material food, that He needed.

There seems no special significance in the varying order of the two remaining temptations, but it is natural to preserve the rising order of importance and to take first the scene on the pinnacle of the Temple. Jesus sees Himself gazing down upon a vast concourse of people. Why not rely upon the word of Scripture and cast Himself down? If invisible angels supported Him so that He alighted on the ground unharmed, would it not at once compel people to believe in His supernatural character? But this would be to misinterpret the spirit of the Scripture and the mind of God. Belief that is forced is no belief at all; there is no moral value in it. There would be only insult in such a testing of divine support. God does not work by magic, and one who would interpret His ways to men must put Him to no such test.

The final temptation comes from the contemplation of the pomp and glory of the world. To accept the value the world places on them would be to worship the devil. No doubt along those lines a person of great gifts and force of character could enjoy an immense success. The world could be His for the asking. But there is a word of Scripture, 'Thou shalt worship the Lord thy God, and Him only shalt thou serve.' He who would save the world must be above the world, even though to save it He must enter into it. He cannot lift the world out of itself unless He places Himself by the side of God; and it is God's methods, not the world's, that He must use.

The devil was defeated. No obscurity clouded the vision of Jesus. The true nature of the Messiahship was clearly seen. All the ancient materialistic trappings of the conception were thenceforth discarded. Jesus saw His goal and the way to it. Not in pomp and circumstance, not with courts and armies, but by self-sacrifice and persuasion, by example and inspiration He would win the hearts of His people, and from that way He would never deviate whatever the consequences might be.

IV. BEGINNING OF THE MISSION

If we can follow the lead of the Fourth Gospel we shall think of Jesus as returning after this experience to the company of John by the Jordan.[1] On three successive days events of importance occurred. On the first John spoke of Jesus as the Lamb of God, and of what he had seen apparently at His baptism. On the second he pointed out Jesus to his own disciples. Two of them, Andrew and probably John the son of Zebedee, began to show a

[1] Jn. 1^{29ff}.

marked interest in Him, and the former introduced his brother, Simeon, to Him. On the third day, which is sometimes reckoned as the first day of Jesus' mission, He started off for Galilee, having first invited Philip and Nathaniel to join His party.

It may seem to us strange that a missioner should be able to collect followers before ever he began to preach. We are expected, however, to take quite seriously the character of the Baptist as the conscious forerunner of the Christ. The view of some modern scholars that the two were rather rivals than helpers has no warrant in Scripture. Indeed the evangelists sometimes appear to forget the sharp division between the teaching of the two, as when St. Luke goes so far as to say that the Baptist actually preached 'the Gospel'.[1] Their presentation of the case makes it possible for us to understand how Jesus came so early to be surrounded by a band of permanent followers. John had pointed to Him as 'He that should come', and had encouraged some at least of his own disciples to attach themselves to Him.

In any case all the gospels agree that Jesus now went to Galilee. Mark tells us that He began to preach in strains very similar to those of the Baptist. 'The Kingdom of God is at hand; repent ye and believe in the Gospel.' But Jesus did at least announce the coming of the Messianic Kingdom as a piece of good news and not merely as a warning of approaching judgment. Matthew tells us that instead of settling down at Nazareth He took up residence at Capernaum. There by the Sea of Galilee He gave a definite call to Simeon, Andrew, James and John to abandon their fishermen's trade and to become with Him 'fishers of men'. The Fourth Gospel tells us that almost immediately ('the third day') there was a

[1] Lk. 3^{18}.

BEGINNING OF THE MINISTRY 51

wedding at Cana of Galilee to which Jesus, His mother and His disciples were invited. There He performed His first miracle and turned the water into wine.

Thus the ministry of Jesus was fairly launched. He had His own circle of disciples, He had begun His own characteristic teaching, and He had already begun to achieve fame as a wonder-worker.

CHAPTER V

GROWING POPULARITY

1. LENGTH OF THE MINISTRY

HAVING seen Jesus launched on His ministry we are now faced with the main biographical difficulty. How long did that ministry last, for one year only or for something over two? As we have already pointed out, the incidents recorded in the gospels were originally narrated as separate stories. They have been assembled there, not necessarily in chronological sequence, but as the purpose or fancy of the evangelist dictated. We therefore cannot rely upon them alone to form an exact judgment of the period covered.

Do the evangelists suggest by their grouping any precise passage of time? Matthew is singularly devoid of any clear indication: he evidently groups his material according to subject-matter, and the time-factor does not enter into his consideration. Mark suggests an early summer in 2^{23} (the ears of corn), an early spring in 6^{39} (the green grass), and (after the visits to Phoenicia, Galilee and Perea) a passover at the period of the Crucifixion. This involves three springs and would demand a ministry of at least two years. Luke collects his material into two masses, one illustrating a ministry in Galilee, the other a ministry in Jerusalem. This could be conceived as occupying no more than one year. It is sometimes thought that Luke's emphasis on 'the acceptable year of the Lord' (4^{19}) does indeed suggest that he thought of the ministry as confined within twelve months or so. Of all the four gospels St. John's is the most precise in the record of time. He gives no fewer than seven dates: 2^{13} a passover (April), 4^{35} a harvest (May), 5^1 Pentecost? (June), 6^4 a passover (April again), 7^2 Tabernacles (October), 10^{22} Dedication (December), and 11^{55} a third passover (April again). This, of course, is decisive for a ministry of at least two years. Or it would be if doubt had not been thrown upon the text in the case of the second passover. The manuscript authority, however, is overwhelmingly in favour of the text as it stands. We shall do well to unite the evidence of the Second and Fourth Gospels and accept the view that our Lord's ministry lasted for a minimum of two years.

The next question is whether there is any possibility at all of finding any chronological arrangement of the incidents between the Baptism and the Passion. Granted that the mention of three passovers gives us a period of two years, can we discover any plausible progress or development in the course of events which would enable us to arrive at any chronological framework in which the bulk of the incidents might be set?

The answer is that there does appear to emerge one allocation of events about the middle of the period which represents a kind of highwater mark of the mission. This is St. Peter's public recognition of the Messianic office of Jesus, followed by the Transfiguration. If this can be taken as the crowning point of success it may be possible to see how other events gradually led up to it, and how still others led down from it, until the final rejection.

Following this general scheme we shall trace the growth of Jesus' popularity, consider the turning-point and then trace the decline of popularity until we come to the Passion narrative itself. This general outline can be taken as established. It has an obvious verisimilitude and something like it might easily have been surmised even if there had been no indications of it in the text. Beyond that it would not be safe to go. The evangelists themselves give us little indication of the order in which they believe detailed events to have taken place. They are content for the most part to use them as illustrating the character of the Christ and His revelation of the Father. We must be content to do the same.

II. FIRST YEAR

The first year seems to have been occupied with a ministry mainly in Galilee, but broken by at least two visits to Jerusalem. The first visit occurred immediately after the events narrated in the last chapter. The Fourth Gospel tells us that Jesus spent a few days at Capernaum with his family and disciples and then went to Jerusalem to be present at the Feast of the Passover.[1] The visit resulted in a considerable number of adherents. They accepted Jesus' leadership on the evidence of the wonders they saw Him perform. Jesus Himself, however, was not satisfied with this. The experience of the Temptation had indeed warned Him against it. Mere intellectual acceptance of His claim without any change of heart was not sufficient.[2]

This is a favourite theme with the fourth evangelist. He enlarges upon it on this occasion by narrating the incident of Jesus' interview with Nicodemus, a Pharisee and member of the Sanhedrin.[3] This man sought Jesus by night and told Him that he was convinced by His miracles that He must be a teacher divinely sent. Jesus, however, put this on one side. The one thing necessary

[1] Jn. 2^{13}. [2] Jn. 2^{23}. [3] Jn. $3^{1\text{ff}}$.

GROWING POPULARITY

was to be born again. It is the spiritual, not the physical, that is truly important. The pronouncement leads into the beautiful discourse, 'God so loved the world', although it is not clear whether these are the words of Jesus or of the evangelist.

Another incident that the Fourth Gospel attributes to this period is the cleansing of the Temple,[1] which the synoptists put at the end of the ministry. The difference illustrates vividly the difficulty we meet in any endeavour to assign a chronological order to these incidents. Some scholars think that even the interview with Nicodemus would be better placed towards the end of the ministry. But for that there is no authority. The synoptists do not mention the incident at all. It is wise for us to stick as close as possible to such authority as we have.

The Fourth Gospel tells us that after this discussion with Nicodemus Jesus went into the country.[2] Evidently He there carried on His mission in much the same way as John the Baptist, who indeed was still at work hard by. Jesus Himself did not imitate John's role of Baptiser, but his disciples did so, and seem to have dealt with even more people than John, whose own baptism was still frequented by great crowds. John's disciples resented the entry of competitors into their field and tried unsuccessfully to arouse John's jealousy. John said that his gradual supersession by Jesus was to be expected. He himself was quite prepared to stand to Jesus as best man to bridegroom: he was only too glad to hear of his friend's success.

Jesus was no more anxious to be adjudged a rival than was John. Rather than allow such a thing to happen He decided to leave Judea and return to Galilee. On the way He passed through Samaria, and it was on this

[1] Jn. 2^{14ff}. [2] Jn. 3^{22}.

occasion that He had His conversation with the woman at the well.[1]

This conversation reveals the universality of Christ's appeal. If He was sent primarily to the lost sheep of the house of Israel, He could still spare time to win over a Samaritan, as later He could deal with a Syrian. It shows too that Christ could make an effort for an individual as well as for a crowd. As in the case of Nathaniel and of Nicodemus, we see how skilfully He handles the situation. He will be put off by no effort to turn the conversation, but will speak direct to the condition of the inquirer, and He knows the circumstances of each one. Nathaniel's inner longing for the life of the Spirit, the matrimonial entanglements of the Samaritan woman—all are well understood by Him and He is able to deal sympathetically with each according to his need. To find Him talking so earnestly to a Samaritan woman occasioned His disciples some surprise. They had yet to learn that He could be equally accessible to children, to lepers and to the outcasts of society.

On His return north Jesus entered upon His first extended tour of work in Galilee. It was preluded by a visit to Cana, where He had performed His first recorded miracle. A 'nobleman' or government official had asked His help for his sick son, but Jesus without even seeing the boy said that he would recover, which proved true. No doubt a naturalistic explanation of such an event is easily possible, but it is narrated by St. John[2] as an instance of Jesus' working of 'signs'. It was His first act of healing. Later we shall have to consider the place of such events in the sum total of Christ's revelatory and redemptive work. For the moment we merely notice it and pass on.

[1] Jn. 4⁷ff. [2] Jn. 4⁴⁶ff.

GROWING POPULARITY

III. WORK IN CAPERNAUM

From the centre at Capernaum on the northern shore of the Lake of Galilee Jesus' fame rapidly spread through the surrounding districts. Unlike the Baptist, who seems to have confined his preaching to the open air, Christ spoke often in the synagogue. There was at first no open breach with the existing religious organisation. As His fame spread, crowds began to follow Him wherever He went. On one occasion He found Himself on the shore of the lake and in imminent danger of being jostled into the water. His friends Simon and Andrew were busy at the time with their boats and nets. Jesus got into Simon's boat, asked him to push out a little and then proceeded to address the crowd from the secure vantage-point of this temporary pulpit. Luke adds to this incident the story of the miraculous draught of fishes. All three synoptists agree that it was on that occasion that Jesus gave a final call, not only to Simon and Andrew, but also to their friends and colleagues, James and John. All alike were fishermen, but there was a difference in their social standing. Simon and Andrew as master fishermen owned their own boats and gear. James and John were in a rather bigger way of business and had hired men to help them. All alike belonged to the Galilean circle that had been profoundly stirred by the apocalyptic and moralistic reform inaugurated by the Baptist. They recognised in Jesus the leader to whom John had pointed. They showed no hesitation in abandoning their work and attaching themselves to Him as disciples and helpers.[1]

Jesus' power as a healer was demonstrated by two further incidents narrated in connection with this tour. At Capernaum Jesus' preaching in the synagogue was

[1] For this incident see Mt. 4^{18ff}, Mk. 1^{16ff}, Lk. 5^{2ff}.

interrupted by a demented person who claimed to recognise Him as the Messiah. This was not the kind of testimony that Jesus wanted. Accepting the current explanation of mental derangement as caused by an 'unclean spirit', Jesus sternly bade the demon to be quiet and to leave the man. The patient immediately passed into a convulsion and was thereafter completely calm. The congregation coupled this personal ascendancy of Jesus over the spirit world with the authority He showed in interpreting the Scriptures. This was in marked contrast to the usual method of the scribes. Their authority was shown in the continual quotation of precedents, His in independent understanding and presentation of the truth.[1]

The other occasion was the healing of Peter's mother-in-law, who was seriously ill with fever. Again, according to Luke, a quiet word was sufficient. Jesus was able to take her by the hand, assist her from her bed, and set her immediately about her household tasks. That evening there was a great crowd of people who were physically or mentally sick surrounding Jesus' lodging and waiting for His healing word or touch.[2] There can be little wonder at the rapidly growing popularity of the new Teacher who displayed such miraculous powers.

But things did not always run so smoothly. There was a set-back in His home town of Nazareth.[3] There He had read the lesson at the service in the local synagogue. The passage was from Isaiah 61. 'The Spirit of the Lord God is upon me; because the Lord hath anointed me to preach good tidings unto the meek; He hath sent me to

---

[1] Mk. 1^{21ff}, Lk. 4^{31ff}.   [2] Mt. 8^{14ff}, Mk. 1^{29ff}, Lk. 4^{38ff}.
[3] Mk. 6^{1ff}, Lk. 4^{16ff}, cf. Mt. 13^{58}. Some commentators think the reason why the congregation was staggered at His 'words of grace' was that He had stopped short of the threat of vengeance against the Gentiles conveyed in Is. 61^2.

bind up the broken-hearted, to proclaim liberty to the captives, and the opening of the prison to them that are bound; to proclaim the acceptable year of the Lord.' These words He applied directly to Himself, emphasising no doubt that His message was to the 'poor'. At first the audience was favourably impressed by 'the grace of His words', although this may mean no more than His eloquence, but when they realised that He was claiming a realisation of ancient prophecy in His own person they turned against Him. In self-defence He described how in the old days Elijah and Elisha had been rejected by their own people and had to perform their miracles among strangers. The congregation could not get over the fact that they knew His family well and that it consisted of local working people. So incensed did they become at what seemed His blasphemy that they rushed Him out of the synagogue with the intention of throwing Him over the cliff. It is true that He escaped their clutches, but the extent of their disbelief made it impossible for Him to use on their behalf the gifts of healing that had been so conspicuous elsewhere. There was nothing for Him to do but to leave the district for a time.

IV. JERUSALEM AGAIN

It is probably at this period that we must insert the journey to Jerusalem mentioned in Jn. 5^1. The feast to which Jesus went with His disciples was almost certainly the Passover. It was made memorable on this occasion by the healing of the paralytic at the Pool of Bethesda. At this pool there was an intermittent spring. It had medicinal qualities, and whenever its waters began to bubble there was a rush of the sick people who lay about in the colonnades, the fancy being that whoever got into the water first was certain to be healed. Jesus' attention had been attracted by a patient who had been ill for a very long time, thirty-eight years. When Jesus asked him whether he would not like to be healed, he replied that he had no one to help him into the water, so he was always too late. Jesus told him to get up and go away. When the Jews saw him carrying his mat they reminded him that it was the Sabbath day and that he was performing illegal labour. With some difficulty they discovered that Jesus was the instigator of this free and easy attitude to Sabbath observance, and started an argument with Him. They were not appeased when Jesus said that He was doing no more than His Father, who as the Sustainer of the universe was always at work, on the Sabbath as on other days. In the eyes of His opponents this reply merely added blasphemy to the offence of law-breaking. St. John regards it as the beginning of definite antagonism on the part of the 'Jews'. He also makes it the occasion of a discourse by Jesus on the relation between Himself and the Father.

A further untoward incident made it unwise for Jesus to remain in Jerusalem. This was the imprisonment of John the Baptist,[1] whose outspokenness had drawn on him the wrath of the king. Herod Antipas, ruler of Galilee and Peraea, had married Herodias, the wife of his half-brother who lived simply as a private person.[2] She was apparently an ambitious woman and had deserted her little-known husband to make a more important match. John openly rebuked Antipas for this offence against the proprieties. He thus incurred the

---

[1] It is possible that this happened during Jesus' previous visit to Jerusalem. See Mt. 14^{3-5}, Mk. 1^{14}, Lk. 3^{19-20}.

[2] St. Mark (6^{17}) appears to confuse this brother with Philip of Iturea, but Philip of Iturea married Herodias' daughter Salome (see below Ch. VII, p. 80).

GROWING POPULARITY

undying hatred of both Antipas and Herodias. They would have had him executed forthwith had not public feeling been obviously in his favour. He was therefore left to languish, as Josephus tells us, in the fortress of Machaerus at the southern end of Perea to the east of the Dead Sea.

Jesus returned to Galilee to find that His fame was now widespread.[1] From Decapolis and Transjordan, and even from Syria, people made pilgrimages to hear him preach and to bring their sick for healing. The case of a man in an advanced stage of leprosy[2] increased His reputation. A dramatic incident at Capernaum led to a break with the Pharisees. Four men had carried a paralysed friend to the house where Jesus was staying. Finding the place so crowded that there was no chance of getting near Him, they had shown sufficient enterprise to get on to the roof, make a hole in it, and lower the man on his sleeping-mat to the feet of Christ. The latter, recognising that the man's spiritual need was even greater than the physical, and appreciating the loyalty and trust of his friends, told him not to be downhearted, for his sins were forgiven. This apparent claim to spiritual authority seemed to the Pharisees a usurpation of the prerogative of God. 'It is blasphemy,' they said, 'Only God can forgive sins.' In order to convince them that He was not speaking idly Jesus told the man to take up his mat and return home: which he at once proceeded to do. But the Pharisees were not likely to forget either Jesus' claim or their own humiliation.[3]

They found further cause for complaint in the company Christ kept. About this time He invited one of the Quisling Jews, Matthew, a man who had entered the

[1] Mt. 4^{12ff}, 23^{ff}. [2] Mt. 8^{1ff}, Mk. 1^{40ff}, Lk. 5^{12ff}.
[3] Mt. 9^{1ff}, Mk. 2^{1ff}, Lk. 5^{17ff}.

service of the Roman authorities as a tax collector or customs officer, to become one of His disciples.[1] When Matthew arranged a farewell banquet to his old associates Jesus did not scruple to attend. It was evident that He did not mean to imitate the exclusiveness of the Pharisees. Nor would He insist upon their hard and fast regulations about fasting. A still further difference became evident when the Pharisees discovered some of His disciples on a Sabbath day walking through a cornfield, plucking ears of corn, and rubbing them in their hands to sift out the grain. This, they said, was the same as reaping and threshing, and was a clear case of breaking the Sabbath. Jesus added to His offence by enunciating the principle that God had not made man to be a slave to Sabbath-day regulations but had ordained the weekly rest to serve the needs of man.[2] The breach with the Pharisees was becoming ominously wide.

V. BEGINNING OF ORGANISATION

With the generality of the people, however, Jesus' popularity was still mounting. So much so indeed that it seemed the time had come to introduce some element of organisation into His mission, and so to extend the scope of His operations. It was the custom of the Sanhedrin, when dealing with ecclesiastical affairs outside Jerusalem, to send appointed representatives who could act as plenipotentiaries or ambassadors to conduct business on its behalf. These emissaries were known as apostles. Jesus determined to adopt the same plan for Himself.

He spends a whole night in prayer, and the next morning calls around Him the closest of His friends and disciples. From them He chooses twelve. The number

[1] Mt. 9⁹ff, Mk. 2¹³ff, Lk. 5²⁷ff. [2] Mt. 12¹ff, Mk. 2²³ff, Lk. 6¹ff.

GROWING POPULARITY

is important and is indeed the name by which this new group was generally known. Twelve was the number of the tribes of Israel, and its adoption would suggest that Jesus recognised Himself as the Messianic King, one of whose functions it was to re-unite the scattered clans. It was probably also the number of the elders who would form the Little Sanhedrin or governing body of any considerable local synagogue.

The Twelve chosen by Jesus were a curiously mixed body.[1] Not all of them attained distinction, and there seems to be some hesitation in the records about even the names of the less known. We can only reconcile the lists by making Levi the same as Matthew, and by identifying Judas with Thaddaeus. Two of them at least have purely Greek names (Andrew and Philip), which suggests that some of the number (and perhaps the Master Himself) could speak Greek as well as the native Aramaic. We have already noticed that there were differences of social standing among them. Such distinction would not count for very much among Jews at that period. But one wonders how such people as Matthew, the ex-tax-gatherer, and Simon, member of the party of Zealots, would get on together. If all were ready to accept Jesus as leader, they would still need much training before they acquired a common mind as to what He had come to do. At least one of them, Judas, the man from Kerioth, never did learn.

It seems natural to take into consideration here, with the First Gospel, the marching orders given to these emissaries of the good news, although the Second and Third Gospels take them later.[2] The scope of the mission of the Twelve is to be strictly limited to Jewish people.

---

[1] Mt. $10^{2\text{ff}}$, Mk. $3^{13\text{ff}}$, Lk. $6^{12\text{ff}}$.
[2] Mt. 10^{1-5}, Mk. 6^{7-13}, Lk. 9^{1-6}.

They are not to deal with Gentiles, or even with Samaritans. They are to travel as light as possible without any change of clothing, and without any financial provision for the journey. They are to rely entirely upon the hospitality with which they may meet on the way. The message they are to deliver is to be precisely that which Jesus Himself had taken up from the lips of the Baptist, 'The Kingdom of Heaven is at hand.' This trumpet-call was to be supported by beneficent wonder-working which would at once suggest their authority as heralds of the Kingdom and exhibit the kindly power of its characteristic life. They were not to press their attentions on unwilling people. If the inhabitants of any township were prepared to listen, well and good; if not, they must be left to their own fate.

To those instructions Matthew adds a discourse (Mt. 10^{16-42}) which in its original intention was evidently meant to apply to some later period when persecution had become rife. Luke on the other hand appends to the call of the Twelve his great example of the Lord's teaching, generally known as the Sermon on the Plain, including the famous Beatitudes and Woes (Lk. 6^{20-end}). This again is closely parallel to the Sermon on the Mount which Matthew gives in another connection (Mt. 5–7). Both discourses are certainly dependent upon the same original. Although they vary greatly in length both begin with the Beatitudes and both end with the allegory of the wise and foolish builders. Scholars are generally agreed that, whatever individual sources they may also have had, both evangelists relied chiefly upon Q, which was a document mainly devoted to our Lord's teaching. It is hardly likely, however, that the discourse was ever delivered wholly as it stands in either version. It falls far too conveniently into various separate pieces

GROWING POPULARITY

for that. No doubt Q had collected together many short sayings of the Master and put them together into one whole, an arrangement which was probably improved upon by both Matthew and Luke. The result was not expected to be regarded as one sermon, but as a compendium either of the Laws of the Kingdom or of the ethical side of Jesus' missionary preaching. For our part we may well follow this example and postpone consideration of these discourses until we come to deal with our Lord's teaching as a whole.

In the meantime Jesus found some tokens of understanding in unexpected quarters. An army officer at Capernaum had a favourite servant lying desperately ill.[1] He persuaded some Jewish elders to invite Jesus' help, and when he found that He was actually coming to the house, he came himself to save Him the trouble, and suggested that a word from Him would be enough. 'I also,' he said, 'am a man *under* authority and so I can give orders myself.' Jesus was amazed at this clear insight on the part of a Gentile into His true character. An order is the expression of a whole system of authority; it can only be effectively given by those who are recognised as within the system. The centurion seems to have realised that Jesus could give orders that would be obeyed just because He was Himself obedient to the Father's will. In any case the soldier's faith was sufficient. He was told to carry on: his servant was healed.

Shortly afterwards, St. Luke tells us, this miracle was followed by another of even greater import.[2] Jesus was approaching the village of Nain, not far from the southeast of Nazareth. As they came near the gate of the village they met a funeral procession coming out. The chief mourner was a widow and the corpse was that of

[1] Mt. 8⁵ᶠᶠ, Lk. 7¹ᶠᶠ.   [2] Lk. 7¹¹ᶠᶠ.

66 THE LIFE OF JESUS CHRIST

her only son. Jesus was deeply moved by the mother's grief and tried to comfort her. Then He put His hand on the bier to stop the bearers, and in the moment's pause told the corpse to rise. The news that Jesus had actually raised to life a dead man spread through the whole countryside and there was more excitement than ever. This is one of the most beautifully told stories in the gospel narrative. For it we are indebted to St. Luke's special source. It is to be noted that in this instance there is no mention of any special faith on the part of the beneficiaries. The miracle arises out of the spontaneous reaction of Christ to human sorrow.

Another lovely story,[1] which probably also comes from St. Luke's special source, although it has certain parallels in other gospels, may serve to end our illustrations of the mounting popularity of Christ. The breach with the Pharisees was not yet complete. One of them even asked Jesus to a meal, although he showed Him little courtesy when He arrived. During the meal a well-known prostitute made her way into the presence of the guests and, weeping bitterly, poured her most precious unguent over the feet of Jesus. Simon the Pharisee was highly scandalised, and all too plainly showed his contempt for one who claimed to be a prophet and yet had not enough insight to see what kind of woman this was. Jesus rebuked him by telling the story of two debtors who were both forgiven their debts. Which of them would show the greater gratitude? Surely the one who owed the greater amount. The sinful woman's moral superiority to the self-righteous host is thus demonstrated. 'Her sins which were many, are forgiven, for she loved greatly; but he to whom little is forgiven loves little.' It is scarcely credible that some commentators treat this as an exercise

[1] Lk. $7^{36\text{ff}}$.

in logic and point out the discrepancy between a love which is the condition of forgiveness and a love which is the consequence of forgiveness. That is just the wrong way in which to interpret a parable. The emphasis of the whole narrative is on the overwhelming character of God's love. To lose oneself in that love is to lose one's sins and to enjoy complete forgiveness.

CHAPTER VI

THE STORY-TELLER

SO far, in trying to gain a comprehensive picture of Christ's life, we have stuck closely to events and incidents, although we have known that there is no guarantee that we have got the detailed events in the right order. It is, however, obvious on a mere glance at the gospels that they are largely taken up, not with events, but with teaching. Later we shall have to give some detailed consideration to the content of that teaching. But already, if we are to gain a proper picture of Jesus as He appeared to His contemporaries, we must give some attention to the way in which the teaching was given.

I. THE PARABLES

It is obvious that Jesus must have presented Himself to the people who came to listen to Him in the guise of a story-teller. A very large part of His discourse is taken up with the stories that we know as the 'parables'. It is quite probable that they occupy in the record a larger proportion of the space than they did in the teaching as actually delivered. Stories are much the easiest part of a homily to remember. In this respect our Lord's sermons were like those of all preachers. At the same time it must be remembered that a story-teller was a popular figure in the East. Anyone who could adapt that style of narration to religious purposes would find plenty of incentive to do so. The fact that Jesus did not shrink from so attractive a method of drawing attention no doubt helped to create for His teaching an

THE STORY-TELLER 69

atmosphere of freshness and of first-hand authority, and to ensure for Him a regular audience.

It would be easy to say that all children love stories and to suggest that child races share the same tastes. The single example of *The Arabian Nights Entertainments* with all that it connotes would be enough to show that there is a special liking for this oral form of narration among Semitic peoples. At the same time the vogue of the short story in our twentieth-century literature would go far to prove that the appreciation of the story-teller's art is not necessarily a sign of immaturity. The Old Testament and the Apocrypha provide us with many examples of the way in which tales were used by the Jews, not merely for entertainment but to point a moral. Round about the period of our Lord's life the method was frequently used by religious leaders. Indeed the Jews are accustomed to regard the Rabbi Hillel as the greatest of all the practitioners of this art.

It is obvious that not all the stories of which we have just been speaking would be recognised as belonging to precisely the same literary form. We must try to understand clearly what is the distinguishing mark of the parable. The schoolboy definition, 'an earthly story with a heavenly meaning', gets very near to the heart of the matter. It does at least bring out the spiritual intention of these stories as used by Christ. But to understand the literary form more clearly we must compare it with a number of closely related styles. Such an examination will perhaps give us a clue to the right way in which to interpret the parables.

II. COMPARISON OF STYLES

The Greek word *parabolé*, which occurs so often in the Synoptic gospels, means literally 'a placing beside for the sake of comparison'. In the Septuagint, however, it is used to translate the Hebrew *mashal*, which is a much wider term including proverbs and aphorisms as well as similes and short stories. If we stick to our own language we can best distinguish the various terms as follows.

The simplest is 'simile', a figure of speech in which one thing is said to be like another. When the two things are kept in juxtaposition without an actual reference to the likeness, the simile becomes a 'metaphor'. Thus 'the moon was like a round cheese in the sky' is a simile: 'The round-cheese moon' is a metaphor. If the simile is expanded into a story without any regard for factual reality it becomes a 'fable'. If the story mingles fact with fancy it is a 'myth'.[1] If, while emphasising the spiritual meaning it keeps close to everyday actuality, it is a 'parable'. In all these instances it is understood that there is just one point of comparison in each story. But if each detail of the story is intended to bear its own point of comparison, then what we have is no longer a fable, a myth or a parable, but an 'allegory'.

It has often been noticed that in the Fourth Gospel, while Jesus is not represented as teaching in extended parables, He is represented as frequently using short similes or similitudes (*paroimiai*). His repeated declaration that He is 'the vine', 'the light', 'the way' will immediately come to mind. It should be noticed that in these instances Jesus does not say that He is *like* the vine, or the sun, or the road. He says that He *is* these things. This may be due to the characteristic directness of Hebrew speech. It may more probably involve a deliberate metaphysical assertion that He is Himself the essential and spiritual reality of which earthly things are

[1] But for the ambiguities still associated with this term see above p. 15.

but the shadows. He *is* the substance: the material existences are but the copies. In any case this type of statement is not confined to the Fourth Gospel. There are examples of these 'proverbs' or shortened parables in the Synoptics; take for instance 'Ye are the salt of the earth', which is expressed in precisely the same form as 'I am the light of the world'. There are others of a looser construction, e.g. 'fields white already to harvest', 'if this be done in the green tree what shall be done in the dry?', 'consider the lilies', 'a reed shaken with the wind'. Any of these could easily be cast into parable form, and it is interesting that the Fourth Gospel consistently prefers the shorter to the longer type. It is this kind of variation that prevents scholars from agreeing about the precise number of parables to be found in the teaching of Jesus.

In tracing the history of the parable in its story form our minds naturally go back to the Old Testament and Jotham's tale of the bramble elected king of the trees,[1] and to the two parables in which David's conduct was reproved.[2] We remember, too, the parabolic forms in which the prophets depicted the relation of Israel to Jehovah, particularly that of the adulterous wife, which reached its culmination in the experience of Hosea. Cruden tells us, in language that could hardly be improved, that the parable 'is a similitude taken from earthly things to instruct us in the knowledge of things spiritual. The parabolical, enigmatical, figurative and sententious way of speaking was the language of the eastern sages and learned men.' There was considerable indignation when the method was employed by charlatans. 'The legs of the lame are not equal, so is a parable in the mouth of fools.'[3]

The method was peculiarly adapted to the Hebrew

[1] Jud. 9^{7ff}.   [2] 2 Sam. 12^2, 2 Sam. 14^2.   [3] Prov. 26^7.

mentality, which was not, like that of the Greeks, at home in abstract, philosophical argument, but dealt naturally with the concrete and personal. Nor were Jewish writers anything like so careful of the precise distinction between associated literary forms as were the creators of classical literature. They could blend simile and allegory in a manner that would have seemed barbarous to a Greek or Roman. Nevertheless they achieved a directness and vividness which the latter could seldom equal, and never excel. Even as a mere literary form Plato's celebrated analogy of the cave can hardly bear comparison with the most ordinary Hebrew parable.

It was natural, therefore, that Jewish teachers should develop the parable as a national style. Whether for the purposes of illustration, argument or straight teaching, these comparative stories were continually on their lips. The phrase 'like unto' became a regular formula of introduction. When the little group seated around Him heard Jesus begin, 'The Kingdom of Heaven is like', they would know at once what form the discourse was going to take and their attention would be riveted upon the story thus announced. As they listened they recognised the voice of a master. His stories dealt with the things they knew: a lost coin, stony soil, a straying sheep, the yeast working in a lump of dough, these were all experiences of their daily lives. If the stories excited their imagination, the moral drawn from them spoke to their conscience. They were stirred to the depths of their being by the authority of a sincere and penetrating word. *Cor ad cor loquitur*. Here was no pedantry or second-hand experience, no word taken from a book, but a direct utterance from primal goodness. 'This man speaketh with authority and not as the scribes.' Of all their teachers This was incomparably the greatest.

III. INTERPRETATION

All this becomes particularly important when we begin to ask ourselves how the parables should be interpreted. We have to remember that Jesus was a Jew and that in matters of rhetoric He belonged to His own national tradition rather than to that of the Greco-Roman world. He was not likely, therefore, to concern Himself with the niceties of logical form. He would not be careful to keep His utterances in meticulously defined categories. As a speaker He was ardent, vivid, direct, ready enough to meet the challenge of the politicians and the intelligentsia, but seeking always the one note of religious sincerity and swift to denounce anything that partook of the nature of hypocrisy. Above all He addressed His teaching to the weary, the frustrated, the soul conscious of its failure and downright sin. It was the moral response that He always sought to evoke.

The recognition of this fundamental fact should help us to answer the most difficult question about the interpretation of the parables, whether they should be treated simply as extended similes or whether they should be treated as allegories. In the former case we shall look for the one main point the speaker desires to make in each story: in the latter we shall look for some added meaning in each separate detail. Thus in the case of the Hidden Treasure, if we adopt the former method we shall fasten our attention on the whole-heartedness of the man who thinks the world well lost if only he can obtain the precious treasure of salvation, but if we adopt the allegorical method we shall begin to ask who is the buyer, what is meant by the field and so on.[1]

---

[1] Good examples of the latter method and its danger can be seen in Ronald Knox, *The Mystery of the Kingdom*. Sheed & Ward.

There is one argument that may seem decisive against the allegorical method. If we enter into such detailed explanations we may soon find ourselves in ethical difficulties. Was it fair for instance for the buyer to conceal from the owner of the field the fact that it contained so great a treasure? Or in the case of the Ten Virgins, while it was right for the wise ones to be prepared, did they not show something less than Christian charity in refusing to share their oil? Such examples suggest that we should not press the parables too far, but should be content in each case with finding the one point and one point only.

This limitation would sweep away at once a great deal of patristic literature, and even of medieval and modern writing, in which the detailed allegorical interpretation of the parables has been pushed to quite grotesque lengths. It would do more. It might even appear to sweep away some parts of our present gospels. Already, in the gospels, we have what looks like an allegorical explanation of some of the parables. Take the Sower for instance. Here we are not only given the salutary lesson that we must continue to sow in spite of some partial failures in the crop, but a lengthy explanation is added in which a personal and psychological interpretation is given of each several kind of soil. Is not this an example of allegorising? If so, where did it originate? It is true that it is put into the mouth of Jesus. But is it likely that Jesus ever explained His own parables, and if He did so would He depart so far from His usually simple and direct method?

Professor Dodd in his fascinating *Parables of the Kingdom* suggests that the explanations come not from Jesus but from the evangelists. Jesus spoke at a particular moment and in respect to a particular situation. But when the evangelists wrote, the moment and the situation had changed. The writers had sometimes lost the point of the original story and they sought an explanation that fitted the circumstances of their own time. That something of the sort may have sometimes happened we need not doubt. For instance at the end of the parable of the Unjust Steward[1] the evangelist seems to be fumbling with three different explanations. He has lost the humour of the original story. It is true that he preserves the all-sufficient comment on the thorough-going practicality of the rascally steward, but he is too serious-minded to be satisfied with the aphorism 'the sons of the world are wiser in their own generation than the sons of light', and adds moralising explanations which confuse the issue.

In view of such aberrations Professor Dodd recommends a completely existentialist interpretation of the parables. Jesus speaks of one situation only at a time, generally that created by the fact that the Kingdom of God has appeared among men and they are in danger of rejecting it. Whatever by way of explanation cannot be made to fit that situation can be safely disregarded as emanating from tradition. It does not belong to the original teaching of Jesus.

This seems to be going too far. Certainly we should always look in the first place for the one main lesson that a parable is intended to illustrate. Where detailed allegorising would lead us away from that lesson, we should unhesitatingly reject it. But where the details extend and reinforce the lesson, there seems no reason why we should not accept the explanation as original. Jesus was not cribbed, cabined and confined within one oratorical form. The extended explanation of the parable of the Sower is so natural, it springs so spontaneously from the necessary answer to an inevitable question, it

[1] Lk. 16$^{1-13}$.

elucidates so admirably the point of the story that the vast majority of readers must surely be astonished to find that in the mind of modern scholars there is any difficulty about it.

IV. PURPOSE

Thus freely interpreted the parables are seen to fulfil the multiple purposes of an accomplished teacher and preacher. They are to be taken as the culmination of the age-long 'wisdom' of the Jews. They cover all the purposes served by those sages, wise men, Rabbis who succeeded to the influence exercised by prophet and priest, and were responsible for the production of the Hebrew 'wisdom literature'. That literature sought to deal with every aspect of life from the nature of God to table manners. So the parabolic teaching of Jesus could include both the highest themes and a half-jesting reference to precedence at meals.[1]

No doubt the main aim of the parable was to arrest attention. Every preacher is conscious of the sudden quickening of awareness on the part of his congregation when he introduces a story into his discourse. But the parable was not just for entertainment, any more than are the illustrations of the modern preacher. It was intended, having riveted the attention of the audience, to face them with the necessity for a decision. The issues of life and death are set before them in a concrete example. On which side are they? Did Simon the Pharisee recognise the gratitude of a man who had been forgiven a debt of 500 denarii to be greater than that of the one who had been forgiven 50?[2] Then he must at once reconsider his attitude to the woman who had stolen into his dinner party and shown such embarrassing devotion to the Teacher.

[1] Lk. 14$^{7-11}$. [2] Lk. 7$^{41-42}$.

A similar aim is seen with particular clarity in those many parables relating to the Kingdom of God. The Kingdom was there, at their doors; were they going to accept it or reject it? The question demanded an answer. There could be no half measures. They must be on the one side or the other, and they must make up their minds now. That was the fundamental issue, and to challenge people to recognise it was the main purpose of the parables.

There were of course subsidiary aims. St. Luke suggests that they taught a hitherto unprecedented care for the 'lost'. In his wonderful 15th chapter he shows that the lost sheep must be sought even if it means the temporary abandonment of the ninety and nine. The lost coin from the married woman's fillet, corresponding to our wedding-ring, causes her more anxiety than all the others she still retains. The lost son breaks his father's heart and his return must be welcomed with every sign of joy, whatever scandal it may cause to the hard and respectable elder brother.

There is, too, the process of gradual enlightenment so nicely proportioned to the slow-dawning comprehension of a people who had hardly penetrated below the superficialities of their national religious observance. As their grasp of reality improved, the more clearly would they be able to understand the essential point of the stories. In this connection a difficulty is raised by the apparent statement of Mark,[1] repeated in Luke,[2] that the purpose of teaching by parables was actually to hide the truth and blind the hearers. It is significant that in Matthew[3] this is changed into an assertion that Jesus spoke in parables because His fellow countrymen were already blinded. The inference is that the only way to teach the people was to present them with 'truth embodied in a tale'.

[1] Mk. 4^{12}.   [2] Lk. 8^{10}.   [3] Mt. 13^{13}.

As they stand the two statements are contradictory. Since we must choose between them, there need be no hesitation in taking Matthew's as more likely to be original. In any case it is not necessary to take Mark and Luke so literally as to make them responsible for the nonsensical view that Jesus spoke in parables in order to hide the truth from His hearers. It is true that to avoid persecution some apocalyptic writers used mysterious symbols in such a way as to reveal their message only to the initiated, and obviously there is more than a suggestion of such *disciplina arcani* here. It is more likely, however, that we have a reminiscence of the passage Isaiah 6[9] where the prophet is bidden to preach to the people and to tell them not to see or hear. In the Hebrew idiom everything that happened was attributed to God's causation and the consequence of an action was regarded as His purpose. *Post hoc ergo propter hoc.* It is probable that Mark slipped unconsciously into this idiom and that Luke with some misgiving followed him, while Matthew corrected him. Indeed Mark himself seems to take the other view in 4[33], 'He spake the word as they were able to hear it.'

The purpose of the parabolic method then was to adapt itself precisely to the capacity of the hearers. From that purpose the stories gained their most characteristic flavour. They proceeded from the known to the unknown, from the familiar to the profound. The events of everyday life are surrounded with a halo of spiritual adventure. The heavenly meaning springs naturally out of the earthly story. There is no wide gap between the material and the spiritual. Nature is seen as the sacramental garment of the hidden mystery. Indeed the whole universe is a sacrament conveying the inner life of God to the soul. This revelation is the challenge of the Kingdom of God.

CHAPTER VII

THE TURNING-POINT

I. THE FATE OF THE BAPTIST

A FORESHADOWING of the fate that might ultimately overtake Jesus in spite of His popularity with the masses could be seen in the persecution of John the Baptist. The document Q, which is used in Matthew 11 and Luke 7^{18-35}, tells us of an incident that happened during his imprisonment, and takes the opportunity to attach to it an estimate by Jesus of His forerunner's work and character.

John's disciples had told him about the wonder-working of the new Teacher, and apparently about the success of His mission. John sent two of them to ask Him the plain question, whether He was or was not the expected Messiah. It is not clear whether John wished to reassure himself or his disciples. Jesus replies in effect that both His works and His teaching show Him to have fulfilled the prophecies in Isaiah 35^5 and 61^1. What more could anyone expect?

We then have Jesus' estimate of John. He was a typical prophet and the greatest of them all, His own forerunner, yet anyone who enjoyed the full blessing of the Kingdom was greater than he. There follows the famous comparison between His own characteristic approach and John's, neither of which has proved acceptable to the Jews. 'You behave like children playing in the streets. John wanted you to play funerals and I wanted you to play weddings, but you wouldn't have anything to do with either of us!' Neither the stern ascetic call of duty nor the warm friendly appeal of love was sufficient to make them face the challenge of the Kingdom.

This incident was followed at no long interval by the death of John.[1] He was actually murdered by order of Herod. As the first two gospels tell the story the murder was engineered by Herodias, who had never forgiven John for his bold denunciation of her second marriage. She watched for her opportunity and gained it when Herod was, in imitation of the Roman emperors, celebrating his birthday feast. At the height of the festivities she sent Salome, her daughter by the former marriage, to enact the part of a dancing girl. This sacrifice of the proprieties demanded a sacrificial gift in return. When Herod told the girl she could have anything she wanted, prompted by her mother she demanded that John's head should be served up as if it were a dish for the feast. Herod, although realising he had been trapped, had gone too far to retract, and the deed was done.

The fact of the murder is vouched for by the Jewish historian Josephus (*Antiquities*, XVIII, 5). But there are differences between his account and that of the gospels. He makes clear that the brother from whom Herod Antipas had filched his wife was not Herod Philip the Tetrarch of Iturea, but another Herod who was at that time living privately in Rome. He also tells us that the reason why Antipas had John put to death was that he feared a political rising on the part of the Baptist's followers. The obvious independence of the accounts shows that we are here in touch with genuine history. The difference as to the identity of Herodias' first husband may arise out of a confusion of names and is of no great consequence. The variation in the reason alleged for the

[1] Mt. 14$^{6\text{ff}}$, Mk. 6$^{17\text{ff}}$.

murder is illuminating. Josephus writes as a secular historian and looks for political motives. The evangelists are religious teachers and are more interested in personal character. There is no reason why on this point both should not be correct. Herod for reasons of public policy would be glad to be rid of John, but hesitated to risk the inevitable outcry. He might not be altogether sorry to be placed in a position where he would seem obliged to give the decision unwillingly.

After the death of John, Jesus with his disciples tried to secure some rest and retirement. The crowd, however, followed them into the country, and hung on His words so long that the disciples became concerned about their lack of food. Jesus would not agree to send them to look for victuals in the neighbouring farms and villages. Had the disciples nothing to offer them? A small boy was produced with his luncheon basket containing no more than five *chapatties* and a couple of sardines. Jesus took these, said grace as any house-father would have done at a family meal, broke the loaves and gave them with the fishes to the disciples for distribution to the multitude. In spite of the fact that the number reached more than five thousand, the food was mysteriously multiplied to such an extent that not only did everyone receive enough, but each of the Twelve was able to fill a basket with the fragments left over.

All four evangelists tell the story[1] and all four are clear that it was a great miracle. By the time they had incorporated it into their narratives it had no doubt been the theme of many recitals and sermons. The evangelists seem to treat it as a lesson to the Church to provide for the material as well as the spiritual needs of the people. The care with which the remains of the meal were

[1] Mt. 14, Mk. 6, Lk. 9, Jn. 6.

collected teaches the need for economy as well as generosity in the distribution of charity.

The first two evangelists give an account later of a similar feeding of four thousand.[1] As the crowd in the first instance was a Galilean one, and that in the second instance was apparently drawn from Decapolis, it has been suggested that the first miracle is symbolic of the mission to the Jews and the second of the mission to the Gentiles. St. John[2] in his distinctive way used the feeding of the five thousand as illustrative of the Eucharist and based upon it the Lord's great discourse on the Bread of Life. Many modern commentators agree that a sacramental feeding is the foundation of the story. But John also, like the others, rests the narrative securely on the basis of accepted fact. He tells us that it roused the multitude to such a pitch of enthusiasm that they tried to take Jesus by force and proclaim Him the Messianic King. Thus interpreted the incident formed the culminating point in the popularity of Christ.

II. TRAINING OF DISCIPLES

To be swept off one's feet by a miracle did not argue any great depth of faith. It was not such a conquest that Jesus wished to win. To have accepted at their face value the acclamations of the multitude would have made His spiritual task more difficult than ever. He therefore withdrew into other regions and, while continuing His normal work, concentrated more and more on the effort to deepen the understanding of His more immediate disciples.

His first step was to send them away by boat in order to free them from contact with the excited crowd, promising to pick them up later. Then, having managed

[1] Mt. $15^{32\text{ff}}$, Mk. $8^{1\text{ff}}$.   [2] $6^{1\text{ff}}$.

THE TURNING-POINT

to disperse the multitude, He spent a good deal of the night in solitary prayer. There followed an unusual incident narrated by Mark, borrowed by Matthew (who added the part about St. Peter) and corroborated by John.[1] It was a stormy night, seas were running high and the disciples were rowing in the teeth of a gale. Suddenly during the fourth watch, that is between 3 and 6 a.m., Jesus appeared walking towards them on the water. Peter with his usual childlike impetuosity said 'Let me do it', but when Jesus called him and he attempted to do it he lost his nerve, began to sink, and had to be rescued by Jesus. Some scholars treat this as a variant of the stilling of the storm (Mk. $4^{35\text{ff.}}$). Others think that it is a parable of the dangers attending the work of Christ's Church, still others that it was preserved as an object lesson for the church in Rome, which was indeed toiling in a dark night just after the martyrdom of St. Peter and St. Paul.[2] We can for our part take it as helping to emphasise the 'numinous' atmosphere surrounding our Lord as He approaches the turning-point of His mission.

Arrived at Capernaum and having again freed Himself from the attentions of the crowd, Jesus began an extended tour through Galilee and on the east side of Jordan into Iturea and Decapolis, and on the west side into the neighbourhood of the coastal towns of Tyre and Sidon. These wanderings gave Him the opportunity for many private talks with His disciples. The Twelve began as a consequence to acquire some measure of confidence in their understanding of His person and work.

An opportunity to test their progress came at Caesarea

[1] Mt. $14^{22\text{ff}}$, Mk. $6^{45\text{ff}}$, Jn. $6^{15\text{ff}}$.
[2] See Rawlinson, *The Gospel according to St. Mark*, p. 88. Methuen.

Philippi. This was the old town of Paneas where there was a temple to Pan. It had been renamed in honour of the Emperor by the tetrarch Herod Philip, and was a place of great natural beauty. Jesus asked the disciples what was the common opinion of Him.[1] They replied that some thought He was John the Baptist, others that He was Elijah, whose return had been promised to herald the Messiah, and others again that He was one of the great prophets, perhaps even Jeremiah himself. 'But who do you say that I am?' 'The Christ,' answered Peter, 'the Son of the living God.'

This represents the highwater mark of appreciation of our Lord's true character. We should not, however, overrate it. It does not as yet imply such a belief in the full deity of Christ as we profess in the Nicene Creed. It is probably little more than a genuine acceptance of Jesus' Messiahship.[2] 'The Son of the living God', the phrase added by Matthew, is a Messianic title. Its emphatic character makes clear the full and complete committal of Peter to the belief expressed. As the first whole-hearted confessor of this faith Peter receives the highest encomium of Jesus. 'Thou art Peter, the rockman, and on this rock I will build My Church, and the fortress of hell shall never defeat it.' To this was added the promise of the keys, the symbol of the steward's office. Peter should have an administrative authority in the Messianic Kingdom and the arrangements he made would be regarded as valid by heaven itself. He would thus take the place of the recognised Jewish authorities, who had misused the power of the keys.[3] It is Matthew who is interested in this question of organisation. Later on he

[1] Mt. 16$^{13\text{ff}}$, Mk. 8$^{27\text{ff}}$, Lk. 9$^{18\text{ff}}$.
[2] 'The Christ' of course means 'the Messiah'.
[3] Mt. 23^{13}, Lk. 11^{52}.

tells us that the same authority was conferred upon the 'disciples' as a whole (18^{18}).

Jesus did not wish much to be made public of this fully established belief in His messianic character, at least for the moment. There was a balancing truth for the disciples first to learn. It was going to be difficult for them to grasp it, particularly when they had just frankly accepted His Messiahship. Nevertheless from that time He began to teach them not so much about the Kingdom as about Himself and especially that He must go to Jerusalem and there suffer and die. This indeed produced a sharp rebuke from the still impulsive Peter, 'That's quite impossible' ('Be it far from Thee, Lord'). But the answer was an equally sharp retort, 'Get out of My sight: you are a positive hindrance to Me: you are completely earth-bound and utterly fail to understand the ways of God'.[1] The disciples still did not understand that the true picture of the Messiah was to be found in the songs of the Suffering Servant.

This was the first clear indication given by Jesus of His certainty of approaching doom. A week was allowed for this teaching to be assimilated by the disciples, and then there occured an incident which gave them the clearest indication they ever had, before that fate overtook Him, of His transcendent character.[2] On one of His accustomed retreats into the mountains for periods of prolonged prayer Jesus took with Him Peter and the two brothers, James and John, that is to say, the three who seem to have been His closest intimates among the disciples. The actual mountain in this case is not identified and speculation on the site is perhaps out of place. It is sufficient to know, not the locality, but the spiritual experience which

[1] Mt. 16^{21ff}, Mk. 8^{31ff}, Lk. 9^{22ff}.
[2] Mt. 17^{1ff}, Mk. 9^{2ff}, Lk. 9^{28ff}, 2 Pet. 1^{16ff}.

Jesus shared with His closest friends. While He prayed the three disciples fell fast asleep. When they awoke they were amazed to see that a great change had taken place in the appearance of their Master. His face was shining with a radiance like that of the sun and His clothes were glittering with an unearthly whiteness. At the same time there were two men talking with Him whom the disciples identified as Moses and Elijah, the great law-giver and the heroic prophet of their national history. They could even hear the subject of the conversation between the three, which was nothing less than the topic that had occupied so much of their own recent thoughts, the death which Jesus had said He must soon meet in Jerusalem. In spite of their terror at the supernatural character of the experience the disciples did not wish it to end. 'Let us make three booths', said Peter with rather more than his usual *naïveté*, so that Jesus and His two visitors could remain and rest. Even as he spoke a bright cloud descended upon them, and out of it they heard a voice, 'This is My beloved Son: see that you obey Him.' At this their fear overcame them and they fell on their faces. The next thing they knew was that Jesus was gently shaking them and telling them not to be frightened. When they looked up the other two had vanished.

Many efforts have been made to find a rationalising explanation for this event. Some scholars have suggested that it really belongs to the post-resurrection appearances and is here misplaced. But it fits in far too well with its context for any such suggestion to be acceptable. It emerges naturally out of the prediction already made of Jesus' approaching death. It is obviously intended to strengthen both Jesus and the disciples for what is to come. The fact that the impending Passion is made the

THE TURNING-POINT

subject of conversation with the two great figures from the past shows that the death of the Messiah is part of the age-long purpose of God. The use of the word 'exodus' by Luke to describe that death links it with the delivery of Israel from Egypt. The descent of the cloud would remind them of the Shechinah or 'glory' of God which so often assured the Israelites of Jehovah's presence with them during the desert wanderings. In the case of Jesus' baptism we have already seen what was the significance of the 'voice' or Bath Qol from heaven. The message was repeated on the present occasion. The emergence of elements from past history into the mental state of a person in an ecstatic condition is a phenomenon well known to psychologists, as is also the effect of such conditions in the physical sphere. He would be a bold man who today would deny the historical reality of the stigmata of St. Francis. It is possible that our Lord's experience was of a similar type. As far as the disciples are concerned the Transfiguration can best be placed amongst those experiences that are classed as 'veridical visions'.

The chosen three were instructed to maintain complete silence about their experience until the events foreshadowed in it had taken place. The moment of exaltation was in any case not likely to last. The next day, when they had descended from the mountain, they found themselves in the midst of an argument between the rest of the disciples and some of the scribes. When Jesus asked what was the trouble, He found that in His absence the disciples had tried to heal a bad case of epilepsy and had failed so ignominiously that the scribes were making fun of them.[1] Jesus asked the father of the sick youth how long he had been subject to the fits. The

[1] Mt. 17^{14ff}, Mk. 9^{14ff}, Lk. 9^{37ff}.

father replied that he had been like that from childhood and added in his desperation, 'If you can do anything, please help us!' 'If!' said Jesus. 'My power to help is in proportion to your faith.' On his profession of belief Jesus complied with the man's request, and, not without terrible convulsions, the youth was healed. The disciples were anxious to know why their own efforts had been unsuccessful. Jesus said it was because of their lack of faith. In any case, He added, this particular kind of demonic possession could only be healed 'by prayer and fasting'. In this last remark some commentators see a reflection of the healing methods of the early Church. The exorcist must be both an ascetic and a man of prayer.

III. FURTHER WANDERINGS IN GALILEE

There followed some further wanderings in Galilee, in the course of which opportunities occurred of enlightening the disciples still more clearly about the character and function of their Master.

At Capernaum the collectors of the Temple tax approached Peter and asked whether Jesus did not pay the tax.[1] Peter answered with some indignation that He certainly did. As he went to get the money, Jesus asked him from whom kings generally collected taxes, their own people or subject folk? The implication was that, as He claimed a special relationship to God, He might be exempt from the payment of contributions for the maintenance of divine worship. However, their actions must not lend any colour to the charge that He was a revolutionary; so they had better conform to custom and pay the tax. If Peter went down to the lake and cast a line he

[1] Mt. 17^{24ff}.

would find a shekel in the mouth of the first fish he caught; that would pay the half-shekel due from each of them.

It is interesting to note that this tax ceased to be payable after the destruction of Jerusalem in A.D. 70. Josephus, however, tells us that it was then appropriated by the Romans for the Temple of Jupiter Capitolinus. It is possible that the narrative as told by Matthew reflects something of the irritation of Palestinian Christians at the situation in which they found themselves. Would they draw the lesson that they must follow the example of their Master and conform even though the temple was now heathen?

The mutual relations of the disciples came under discussion when Jesus discovered that they had been arguing among themselves which of them should occupy the chief position in the Messianic Kingdom.[1] He told them that the sign of true greatness is service to others. He enforced the lesson by setting a little child in their midst and explaining that the man who most deeply cultivated the childlike mind would rank highest. How difficult it was to learn this lesson was to be seen later when the mother of James and John actually asked Him to promise that her sons should occupy the most important posts when He had established His Kingdom.[2] His reply on that occasion was that they should have the privilege of sharing in His sufferings; posts in the Kingdom, however, were not His to give, but the Father's.

Relations with outsiders were set in a new light when John said he had found an exorcist using Jesus' name as a charm to drive out demons, and because he was not actually a follower of Christ, had forbidden him.[3] Jesus said this was the wrong attitude to adopt. They should

---

[1] Mt. 18^{1ff}, Mk. 9^{33ff}, Lk. 9^{46ff}. [2] Mt. 20^{20ff}, Mk. 10^{35ff}
[3] Mk. 9^{38ff}, Lk. 9^{49ff}.

not stop such people: that would only drive them into opposition. What they should do was to regard everyone not actively opposed to them as on their side.

This series of instructions culminates in the reply to Peter about forgiveness.[1] Peter no doubt thought he was putting the possibility of repeated forgiveness very high when he suggested that one could do it seven times. In the Hebrew idiom seven was the perfect figure, a good round number. But Jesus said one should be ready to do it seven times a day, and if necessary to a total of seventy times seven. That of course meant that one should go on doing it so long as there was any chance of bringing the offender to a better mind. It is obvious that forgiveness is not used in the mere negative sense of readiness to forget, but in the positive sense of a creative activity which is bent on the complete restoration of the wrongdoer.

It was now late September or early October of the year A.D. 28. The Feast of Tabernacles, a sort of Harvest Festival, was soon due to begin. Jesus' relatives urged that He should keep it in Jerusalem.[2] They had very little faith in His claims, indeed they thought that He was suffering from some mental derangement which manifested itself in what they no doubt considered His megalomania. But they were not above challenging Him to show Himself off in Jerusalem. He told them that boastful displays were more in their line than His, and He let them go off without Him. He was, however, fully aware that He could not escape His own crisis, and He proceeded to follow as quietly as He could, avoiding the main route and travelling by side roads.

He met with a mixed reception on His passage through Samaria.[3] At a border village ten lepers who had heard of

[1] Mt. 18$^{21\text{ff}}$, cf. Lk. 17$^{3-4}$.   [2] Jn. 7$^{1\text{ff}}$.   [3] Lk. 17$^{11\text{ff}}$.

THE TURNING-POINT

His reputation asked for healing, but when the request was granted only one of them had the grace to delay long enough to thank his benefactor. He, as it turned out, was a Samaritan. But later, when Jesus' party tried to arrange accommodation, the Samaritans refused to receive them on the ground that they were obviously going to Jerusalem.[1] James and John, 'sons of thunder', were so angry that they would have liked to call down fire from heaven to annihilate them, but Jesus reproved the two brothers and led His disciples quietly on to another village.

Arrived in Jerusalem He early discovered that He was the main topic of conversation, and that opinion about Him was very divided. This was so even among the ordinary people, who did not seem able to make up their mind whether He was a good man or an impostor.[2] In any case they were afraid to discuss Him openly because of the priests who were set against Him. When He began to defend Himself they were amazed at His skill in argument. Did they accuse Him of breaking the Law, they were not immune from the same charge themselves. Did they accuse Him of healing on the Sabbath, they were asked whether that was any worse than performing the operation of circumcision on the Sabbath. Did they complain that they knew His family while that of Messiah would never be known, the answer was, 'Yes, they might know His family, but they did not know the heavenly source in which His mission originated.' None of this made the authorities any happier about Him. They began to foster thoughts of His arrest.

The Feast of Tabernacles ended with ceremonies concerned with water and lights. It was in this connection that Christ preached His sermon on the water of the Spirit, 'If any man thirst let him come unto Me and

[1] Lk. 9$^{52-53}$.   [2] Jn. 7^{10ff}.

drink', following it with another on 'the Light of the World', and supporting it with the healing of the blind man at the Pool of Siloam.[1]

These events brought the division of opinion to a head. The Jewish authorities thought the moment was opportune to make an arrest. They sent officers to apprehend Him,[2] but the officers listened to His preaching and lost heart in the business. They returned empty-handed, and frankly revealed their admiration for the Preacher. Their masters accused them of allowing themselves to be taken in. When one of the Sanhedrin, the Nicodemus who had once gone to Jesus by night, expostulated against assuming that a man was guilty before he had even been examined, they rounded on him too. 'Another of these Galilean fanatics. If you would only read the Scriptures you would see that no prophet ever came out of Galilee.' This meant that the die was cast. Henceforth there was to be no peace between Jesus and the Jewish authorities. It was to be an opposition to the end.

[1] Jn. 7, 8, 9.   [2] Jn. 7^{32-45}.

CHAPTER VIII

THE TEACHER

1. JESUS' DOUBLE WORK

JESUS had two tasks to perform. He had to make known the true character of God and He had to rescue men from the ineffectiveness and sin into which they had fallen. It was of course impossible to keep these two functions of revelation and redemption in watertight compartments. God would be revealed not only by His words but by His life, and specially by that part of it which was most obviously concerned with the redemption of humanity. Conversely man would be redeemed not only by the atoning acts of Christ, but also by His persuasive words. Nevertheless it is possible to consider the two functions separately, and it may help us to get a clearer grasp of the life of Christ if we consider His work as teacher in isolation.

The term teacher is a comprehensive one, and for our purposes it must be taken to include not only our Lord's actual instructions, but also His preaching and His story-telling. With the last of these three we have dealt in a separate chapter, so that we are left here with the teaching, strictly so called, and the preaching. It seems that the latter was the earlier in time. The Greek word for preaching implies strictly the proclamation of a herald, and preaching always has retained the character of an announcement. The gospel was itself 'good news', and it had to be proclaimed before any detailed instruction upon it could be given. So long as the synagogues were open to Him, we picture Jesus using the opportunities afforded to a new Rabbi of expounding the Scripture in the weekly service in order to proclaim, 'Today is this word fulfilled in your ears.' This proclamation of the advent of the Kingdom sums up our Lord's task as a preacher.

As a teacher our Lord presents a different picture. We see Him seated in some open space or on some point of vantage, such as the prow of a ship or a jutting rock, talking and telling stories to the people gathered around. When He began to lose His popularity and the synagogues were not so readily accessible to Him He would rely more and more on this method of presenting His message.

The people who listened to Him were mostly of the peasant class, but this does not mean that they were necessarily ignorant or illiterate. The Jews used their synagogues as schools, and as everyone had to learn a trade, so everyone was expected to imbibe a modicum of education. The difference of intellectual attainment and of practical capacity between one class and another was therefore a good deal less obvious than it is among ourselves. At the same time there would generally be among His hearers a certain number of scribes and lawyers, professional casuists, who were always interested in a new teacher, and particularly anxious to discredit one who did not measure up to their standards or who produced disturbing novelties. There can be no doubt, however, that Jesus' most intimate and detailed teaching was given privately to the inner circle of His disciples. Indeed it has even been suggested that this esoteric teaching may be responsible for the special character of the Fourth Gospel as distinct from the Synoptics.

Neither the preaching nor the teaching of Jesus was given on systematic lines. Really it would have been quite unlike what we know of Him if He had dealt with His subject after the manner of a professor in the lecture room. If there ever appears even a slight approach to a systematic treatment in the gospels, it is probably because the evangelists have imposed some sort of order upon the many fragments of discourse they have pieced together. Matthew, it is true, appears in the Sermon on the Mount to be presenting a picture of Christ as a new Moses promulgating the law of the Kingdom from a new Sinai. But even there Jesus speaks more like Moses the prophet.[1] Indeed both types may be transcended if we see in the Beatitudes a series of aphorisms even more like the utterances of the typical Jewish 'Wise Man'. These sayings may be compared with the collections found at greater length in the Wisdom Literature, such as Proverbs, Wisdom, Ecclesiasticus.

Some have found in the discourses of Jesus a style closely resembling that of a poet. Certain it is that large sections of His discourse when translated back from the Greek into what was presumably its original Aramaic fall easily into verse rhythm. It has been suggested that the Lord in His prophetic utterances habitually dropped, like a Welsh preacher or a French orator at the height of declamation, into a rhythmic intoning which would much more closely resemble poetry than ordinary conversational prose. If this is true, then we have here an extraordinarily vivid illumination of the actual conditions under which Jesus conducted His ministry.

What most struck His contemporaries about His teaching was the direct authority with which it was given. People compared Him with the professional Rabbis.

[1] 'In the Sermon Jesus gave His disciples not so much a new law (though Matthew's presentation of it may well give that impression) as a design for living.' A. M. Hunter, *The Work and Words of Jesus*, p. 67. S.C.M.

They too spoke with authority, but their authority was that of the scholar, dependent upon the earlier authorities he can quote and compare. Christ leaned only upon 'the singularity of His own wit'. He spoke as one who had a right to be heard for what He was. In this respect He went even further than the prophets. They prefaced their most solemn pronouncements with 'Thus saith the Lord', but Jesus opened even His contradictions of the Law with a simple 'I say unto you'.

II. THE KINGDOM

It was in this spirit that Jesus made His proclamation of the coming of the Kingdom. This was the main, the fundamental subject of His preaching at least in the earlier part of His ministry. Nothing could show a clearer departure from a true understanding of the New Testament than the attempt to substitute for this proclamation some nineteenth-century teaching of ethics. The great thing that Jesus proclaimed was the gospel of the Kingdom, the good news that the long-expected Messianic reign was on the point of appearance. He did not originate this message. He took the text from the mouth of the Baptist, who had inaugurated his reform in order to prepare the people to receive the Kingdom and enter into it when it came. Jesus proclaimed the same message in louder and more ringing tones. Presently, however, He alters it. After the confession of belief in Him as Messiah by Peter at Caesarea Philippi He proclaims that the Kingdom has already come, and leads people to understand that as they associate themselves with Him they have already entered into it. However bizarre this announcement may seem to us, and however remote from the sober judgment of a level-headed reformer, one has no right to tone it down. To such of His contemporaries as accepted it, it seemed epoch-making. To those who did not accept it it seemed the most dangerous imposture; and it was for this reason that they hounded Him to His death. However little or much the announcement of the Kingdom means to us, to Him it was a matter of life and death, both for Himself and for the world. His announcement of it was therefore the greatest and most peremptory of all possible challenges.

Since the idea of the Kingdom was so fundamental to the preaching of Jesus it may seem surprising that we have no carefully articulated theology of it. In this it is rather like the subject of the Atonement, about which there has been much research, but no official dogma. In the case of the Kingdom there has been a great revival of interest in recent years, provoked no doubt by the successful appeal of several secular Utopias, most of which borrowed some of their essential features from the idea of the Kingdom taught by Christ. We are able now to recognise some of the mistakes we have made in presenting the doctrine of the Kingdom. Our failure has opened the way for the perversions of Fascism, Nazism and Marxism. We have interpreted the Kingdom as an apocalyptic vision which can only be realised in the future. Or we have individualised the whole conception as if it had no interest for the community as a whole. Or we have made the very conception unnecessary by identifying it with the Church.

In correction of these and suchlike mistakes there are three points in Jesus' teaching of the Kingdom which stand out as specially important. First, the completed Kingdom is the ultimate goal of history. St. Paul was adequately interpreting the teaching of his Master when he said that Christ would reign till He had subdued all enemies under His feet and that then He would hand over His Kingdom to the Father so that God might be all in all (1 Cor. 15). If the Kingdom is thus to be the fulfilment of all earthly life it obviously gives a meaning and purpose to our present existence. We are here to fit ourselves and our surroundings for it. Preparation for it should be the dominant note of every life.

From this it follows in the second place that the Kingdom is the perfect society. This includes of course our so-called secular activities as well as our specifically religious or ecclesiastical interests. The ends of the Kingdom must be pursued in the home and in the workshop as well as in the Temple or the synagogue. It is true that Jesus said, 'My Kingdom is not of this world', but by this He meant that He was not seeking an earthly throne with the aid of armed forces.[1] Later writers drew out the implication of His teaching for society. As Moses constructed the Tabernacle after the pattern shown him 'on the Mount', so we must make our civic and national organisation conform to the perfect pattern in the Kingdom of Heaven.

Thirdly from this it follows again that the Kingdom begins for each individual within the circle of his own personality. The Kingdom of God is not only the goal of history and the perfect society, it is also the rule of God in men's hearts and lives. Jesus taught that the Kingdom had already been introduced into the world with Himself. People entered it when they were linked with him. It would be established with power by stages in various great events and historical occasions. His followers realised that they could not themselves command the coming of the Kingdom: it was something only God could give. But they could prepare the way for it in their own

[1] Jn. 18^{36}.

lives and in their environment. In the end it would appear as the holy city, new Jerusalem, descending from God out of Heaven.[1]

III. THE CHURCH

It must be admitted that in comparison with the Kingdom Jesus seems to have had little to say about the Church. Twice St. Matthew records that He mentioned it in specific terms, once when He told His followers to bring their quarrels for settlement to the Church (18^{15-18}), and once when Peter had confessed belief in His Messiahship and He said, 'On this rock will I build My Church' (16^{17-19}). In both cases it is often alleged that the evangelist was incorporating into the actual teaching of Jesus elements from the later experience of the Christian community. This is probably a gratuitous assumption.

In any case we have abundant evidence that Jesus attributed first-class importance to the constitution of the 'little flock' to whom He promised the Kingdom. He regarded them as the faithful remnant of the old people of God, the New Israel, which had now become, through the failure of the nation as a whole to realise its opportunity, the inheritor of the Old Testament promises and blessings. The fact that admission to its membership by the rite of baptism was universally associated with the name of Christ cannot be ignored. At the Last Supper He established the New Covenant with another characteristic rite. He carefully trained His disciples and organised the Apostles as the ministerial nucleus of the society which would continue after His own departure from the earth. If we may accept the report of the Fourth Gospel

[1] I am aware that the above is a very inadequate treatment of a large subject, but I must refer the interested reader to my brochure *The Mystery of the Kingdom.* Faith Press 1953.

He announced that His association with the members would be as close as that between the vine and its branches, in both of which flowed the same sap, the same vital energy.

Of course, all these traditional assertions have been submitted to the severest examination, and many alternative explanations have been offered. But these explanations are for the most part invented in order to escape the obvious New Testament teaching, that Jesus did intend the continuance of an easily recognisable society now associated with Himself. That society had its roots in ancient history. It had already existed for centuries in the Israelite nation, but in Jesus it was purged, reformed and given a new start. The Christian Church was the child and the replacement of the Jewish Church.

The Church thus conceived was not an end in itself. It existed for a specific purpose, and had a specific duty to perform. That was to prepare the way for the coming of the Kingdom. In the nature of the case it was inevitable that Church and Kingdom should be to some extent confused. They certainly overlapped. The Church was the nucleus of the Kingdom. It inevitably became a clearly defined ecclesiastical organisation with its own officers, its own rites of admission and membership, its own rules of conduct and belief. All that was not yet. But it was inherent in the Lord's appointment of the Twelve, in His use of Baptism and in His institution of the Lord's Supper.

IV. GOD

Jesus came proclaiming the Kingdom. He also came revealing the Father. Consciousness of God and of God as Father was the most conspicuous element in the thought of Jesus. He made His hearers understand that God was no stern judge or capricious tyrant, but a dependable Creator and Sustainer of the universe, whose essential nature was love. The Father knew every hair on the head of each individual and cared for the fate even of the odd sparrow that had been thrown in for luck when five birds were sold for two farthings.[1] Sin and folly could not destroy the love He felt for each of His children. He sought the lost sheep and awaited the return of the Prodigal Son.

Complete, whole-hearted devotion to His Father was the dominant note in Jesus' own character. He was so closely in touch with Him that in His first miracle at Cana of Galilee He could say at one moment that 'His hour was not yet come' and at the next could bid the servants fill the water-pots with water and the miracle was performed. Jewish teachers had often spoken of God as Father, but normally they thought only of their own nation as His children. Jesus extended the conception to include all human beings. If sometimes, as for instance to the Syro-Phenician woman, He spoke as if His own mission was confined to Israel, it was either to test the faith of His hearers or to suggest that even He must do one thing at a time, and must content Himself in the present with the preparation of those who would carry out the universal mission after His death.

It is sometimes suggested that while Jesus taught only about His Father, later generations altered the balance of His teaching and taught almost entirely about Jesus. It is thus affirmed paradoxically that 'Christianity' was not the religion of Jesus. There is, of course, a certain element of truth in this, but it would be quite untrue to assert that Jesus had nothing to say for Himself. The use of the title

[1] Lk. 12⁶.

Son of Man[1] must be accepted, not merely as an affirmation of humanity, but as a claim to the title of Messiah. It is true that Jesus, like every good teacher, tried to lead His disciples to recognise the truth for themselves rather than force it upon them by the weight of His authority. He had His reward when Peter acknowledged His Messiahship at Caesarea Philippi. 'Thou art the Son of God, Thou art the King of Israel.' But He had effectively made that claim for Himself when He identified Himself with the Suffering Servant of the songs from 'Isaiah'.[2] Whether those songs originally referred to some historic person, or to an ideal Israel, or to the faithful remnant, we may never know. What is certain is that the dominant note in them is that of vicarious suffering. Jesus made it clear that in His conception the Messiah would be no glittering warrior, but one who would save His people by suffering for them. And He made it abundantly clear that He conceived Himself to be that one. This involved a revolution in the popular notion of the Messiah. No wonder that His disciples were slow to grasp the truth. The fact that they did so at last is sufficient testimony to Jesus' skill and gentleness as a teacher.

Of His task as Redeemer Jesus inevitably had much to say. He had come to save His people from their sins, and, as we have seen, He gave a wider connotation to the term 'people' than the purely national one. Further, He obviously regarded all men as sinners, not least those who were blind to their own faults. All men alike therefore were the objects of His redeeming Love, as they were of the Father's. If Jesus Himself was the Good Shepherd, God was the Father of the Prodigal. But there

---

[1] See the final chapter for consideration of this and other titles.
[2] See especially Isaiah 49, 53.

was no easy way of restoring the ideal relation between man and God. It was not that God was not ready to forgive, but that man was not ready to be forgiven. He was too deep under bondage to sin for that. He must be bought back, redeemed, from such slavery. It was precisely for that purpose that He Himself had come. He had come to give Himself a ransom for many.[1] When He had paid the price, the movement of penitence (the *metanoia*, the change of mind) would begin to work in their hearts and the way to forgiveness would be open.

According to the Fourth Gospel this redemptive character of the work of Christ was seen by His forerunner from the beginning. The Baptist actually hailed Him as 'the Lamb of God that taketh away the sins of the world'.[2] He thus indicated that in Christ was to be fulfilled the whole history and intention of the Jewish sacrificial system. Jesus' sacrifice of Himself would be the real atonement for sin and the means of establishing righteousness. Whether this assertion on the part of the evangelist was factual history or intelligent anticipation, it is certain that Jesus accepted this view of His life and work. Not only did He appropriate to Himself the songs of the Suffering Servant which taught the same moral lesson, but at the Last Supper He used language about His body, now to be given for His disciples, which demands the same explanation. In His words about the new covenant in His blood He proclaimed that He must die in order that Jeremiah's prophecy about the new covenant, written in the hearts of God's people rather than on tables of stone, might adequately be fulfilled. If repentance—a sorrow for the past, and, for the future, a readiness to accept the gift of God's grace with the trustfulness of a child who can earn nothing for itself

[1] Mk. 10^{45}. [2] Jn. 1^{29}.

but only receive—if repentance such as that was the only way to forgiveness, then this, the death of Christ, was the only way to repentance.

V. CONDUCT

As for the way in which the citizens of the Kingdom were to live in this world, Jesus, without promulgating any detailed code, did proclaim a revolutionary principle of ethics. He struck at the roots of man's pride in his own attainment and made him completely dependent upon God. Man could not attain virtue or merit for himself. On the contrary, he must *accept* a new life and then live it out in his daily affairs. All the virtues that Christ extolled in the Sermon on the Mount are the expression of a character created within each individual by the new relationship with God.

The propulsive power in this new life is love. This is what the old Law had been leading men towards. It is summarised in two propositions: 'Thou shalt love the Lord thy God with all thy heart, with all thy mind, with all thy soul, and with all thy strength, and thy neighbour as thyself.' But the two loves are not the same. The love of God is adoration and self-surrender; the love of man is pity and desire to help. Or as someone has said, 'the love of God is passion, the love of man is compassion'. The first is easy to understand, if not easy to encompass. The second has not even been understood. The usual word *agape*, used to express it, was certainly selected to make its special character obvious. 'A new commandment,' says our Lord in the Fourth Gospel, 'I give unto you that ye love one another, even as I have loved you.'[1] Our attitude to our fellow-man is not to be dictated by

[1] Jn. 13:34.

fluctuating emotion. It has nothing to do with liking or disliking. It is the steady set of the will to do the best we can for every individual with whom we come into contact, whether friend or foe. It is the governance of the whole life by the determination to serve the highest interests of each and all with whom we have to do.

In general our Lord's demands on His disciples are stated in the most absolute terms. We are not to resist evil, but turn the other cheek. We are to be poor, meek, peacemakers, childlike. The unity of husband and wife is to be complete: there is to be no divorce. (The 'Matthaean exception' is now generally agreed not to have been uttered by Jesus.) For His sake we must be prepared to surrender everything—wealth, family, personal ease. We are to 'hate' father and mother; go to the stake ('take up the cross') every day. These requirements surpass all political considerations. It is perhaps hardly surprising that one political theory after another has found justification for itself in the teaching of Christ—anarchism, communism, socialism, capitalism, democracy, autocracy—all alike have found something in the gospels to support their own panacea for the ills of the world. But they have been able to do so only by neglecting other elements of the teaching, just as strongly expressed, which do not fit in with their views. Jesus as a teacher adopted the plan of stating one thing at a time and stating it as clearly as possible. He was not perturbed by any seeming inconsistency or even contradiction in what He said on two different occasions. He was thus able to deal in absolute values without qualification or equivocation.

Schweitzer and his followers maintain that Jesus was able to adopt this absolute standard in all sincerity only because His ethics were 'interim' ethics. They were intended only to cover the very short period He expected to elapse between the contemporary moment and the appearance of the Kingdom of Heaven, which was to be ushered in by His death. For so short a time His followers could be expected to live on the level of perfection. This theory has been abandoned with the general rejection of the purely apocalyptic interpretation of Christ's eschatology. There is no doubt that these were the ethics of the Kingdom itself and not of some interim period. Since we now recognise that in Him the Kingdom had already dawned and there was no interim period, it follows that these were the ethics by which the Church was expected to live in perpetuity.

Could it be then that the ideals were of only partial application? Were some intended for one set of people and others for another? Was there a difference, as later Christians began to teach, between counsels and precepts? Or were there two different standards of attainment, one necessary for mere salvation the other necessary for perfection? Jesus told the rich young ruler that what he needed was to sell all his goods and give to the poor. It is hardly likely that He intended this advice to be of universal application. Jesus refused to adopt the role of an ascetic: that, He said, had been the function of the Baptist. Yet He demanded self-discipline in the strongest terms. He did not lay down a universal celibacy (or teetotalism!). Yet He said that there were those who adopted such an ideal for 'the Kingdom of Heaven's sake.' What is the solution of the apparent inconsistency? It seems that in Jesus' view each person has his own individual vocation. It is not a question of two standards. There is only one standard for us all and that is perfection. But perfection in each case consists in obeying God's will for oneself. Each must pursue the absolute demand as adapted to the circumstances of his own life.

One further thing may be said. Those are truly the ethics of the Kingdom. But the Kingdom of God is an irruption of eternity into time. The ethics are the absolute ethics of eternity. We must carry them out to the fullest possible extent in our own situation. That situation is twofold. If we have become citizens of the Kingdom of Heaven we are still denizens of this world of space and time. We must so conduct ourselves in those ambivalent circumstances as to ensure the speediest possible fulfilment of the demands of the eternal law. A tremendous responsibility is placed upon the individual. But if he is afraid or diffident, he must remember that he is already a citizen of the Kingdom and as such is already endowed with the power of eternal life.

CHAPTER IX

THE PERIOD OF OPPOSITION

1. MISSION OF SEVENTY AND ITS RESULTS

WE left Jesus at the close of the Feast of Tabernacles facing the avowed and open opposition of the Jewish authorities. There was to be no reconciliation, but the end was not yet. Even in these very unfavourable circumstances Jesus felt Himself strong enough in popular support to send out another mission to the countryside.[1] This was on a bigger scale than that of the Twelve, no fewer than seventy messengers being employed. They were sent out two by two into the villages which Jesus intended Himself to visit later. The instructions given them bear a close similarity to those given earlier to the Twelve. The seventy are to rely upon local hospitality, and they are to return that hospitality by healing the sick. The subject of their preaching is to be the same as that of Jesus and the Twelve, namely the challenge of the Kingdom of God. They are to speak with the authority of Christ Himself, and they are to be stern with those who will not receive them, or accept their challenge.

In due course they returned, and they gave a very happy report of their success, particularly in their work as exorcists. On hearing the news Jesus enjoyed one of His few moments of ecstatic joy. It was to Him a glimpse of Satan's fall from heaven. It was a foretaste of the final victory of good over evil. Commentators believe that to this incident belongs the passage (Mt. 11$^{27-30}$) in which

[1] Lk. 10$^{1\text{ff}}$.

THE PERIOD OF OPPOSITION 109

Jesus thanks the Father that He has reserved this revelation for the babes rather than for the worldly wise, and that He has Himself been chosen to be its vehicle. And then He apostrophises the needy with His gracious invitation: 'Come unto Me, all ye that labour and are heavy laden, And I will give you rest.'

While Jesus' popularity with the common people was thus as strong as ever, the breach with the professional classes was continually widening. One whom St. Luke in his characteristic way calls a 'lawyer',[1] asked Jesus what he must do to make sure of eternal life. Jesus gave him an answer out of his own Scriptures, 'Love God and your neighbour.' The lawyer tried to justify himself by asking, 'Yes, but who exactly is my neighbour?'. To this Jesus gave no direct reply, but told a parable of a Samaritan who alone was found to show himself neighbourly when both priest and Levite had glaringly failed. The lesson intended to be learnt is that we must not lose ourselves in academic theorising but get on with the business of *agape*, of constant service of all who cross our path.

On another occasion, when Jesus had been engaged in prayer, His disciples asked Him to teach them how to pray.[2] In response to their request Jesus gave them as a pattern the prayer which St. Matthew introduces into the Sermon on the Mount[3] and which is to be found with minor variations in St. Luke. They were told that prayer was not to be a mere constant repetition of a fixed formula like that of the prophets of Baal (1 Kings 18^{26}) or of the contemporary Pharisees (Mk. 12^{40}: Lk. 20^{47}). Our prayer should always be mindful of God's honour and

---

[1] Lk. 10^{25}. He was writing for Gentiles and used this term where the other evangelists would say 'scribe'.
[2] Lk. 11$^{1\text{ff}}$. [3] Mt. 6$^{7\text{ff}}$.

the need to fulfil His will. In that context only should it ask for the satisfaction of both material and spiritual needs. It was customary for Rabbis to compose a special prayer for their pupils. The Baptist had evidently done the same for his disciples. But none ever combined in their pattern prayers the simplicity and sublimity of the Lord's Prayer. Its opening words 'Our Father' broke down all personal isolation and united the disciples in a common approach to God, not as King or Judge, but as their common Parent, thus making them at home in the universe and reminding them of the friendliness of Heaven. The petition for the speedy establishment of the Kingdom kept the goal of life constantly before them and reminded them of their duty to prepare the way for its coming. The petition for 'daily bread' made them realise the interest of God in their physical welfare and kept before them the importance of little things. To some commentators, both ancient and modern, this has been a stumbling-block and they have taken the unusual word rendered 'daily' to mean 'heavenly' or 'super-essential'. There can now, however, be no doubt what was its significance in the common speech of that day. It has been found in a papyrus containing a housekeeper's accounts, and there it can only mean the daily ration, the bread for each day. The petition 'Lead us not into temptation' squarely faces man's spiritual need and prevents any mock heroics. No one should wish to be led into any situation that involves a grave inducement to sin, but should desire at all costs to avoid moral evil. That concludes the original prayer. The doxology was probably added from later liturgical forms.

The prayer was undoubtedly used from the first in Christian worship, and it is notoriously difficult to maintain the purity of texts in constant liturgical use,

THE PERIOD OF OPPOSITION

witness the alterations that are always taking place in popular hymns. The same cause may well account for the difference between the Lucan and Matthean forms of the prayer. Even in living memory, in spite of all the modern aids in printing and proof-reading, the precise punctuation of the prayer has been the subject of hot debate in the House of Commons. In any case it is always possible and even probable that our Lord Himself gave His model at different times and in different forms. It was the spirit rather than the precise words that He wished to inculcate.

If the disciples were to avoid the use of 'vain repetitions' they were nevertheless to be persistent in their prayers. Luke adds to the teaching of the pattern prayer the amusing story of the importunate friend who wants a couple of loaves for an unexpected visitor and insists on getting his neighbour out of bed to lend them.[1] Those who are sufficiently earnest in their prayers can be assured that they will be answered and that they will get whatever a wise Father knows is best for them.[2]

Jesus' fame as a wonder-worker, paradoxical as it may seem, brought Him fresh difficulties. Q gives us some instances of the trouble caused by His works of healing. The crowd could not be sure whether the miracles were not the result of diabolic influence. Jesus had been casting out a 'dumb spirit' when some of the witnesses asserted that He could do such things only because He was in league with Beelzebub.[3] But how ridiculous that would be, He answered; it would imply that Satan was fighting against himself. In any case your own people sometimes effect the same cures. Would it not be easier to believe that My special gift in this respect

[1] Lk. 11⁵ff. [2] Lk. 11⁹ff, cf. Mt. 7⁷ff.
[3] Mt. 12²²ff, Lk. 11¹⁴ff.

is a sign that the Kingdom has already come? You ought to be fighting with Me in this campaign. You can't sit on the fence, and if you don't range yourselves on My side you are in effect fighting against Me. By the same token I would warn all those who have been healed to occupy themselves with the furtherance of the Kingdom. If they fall into idleness it is quite possible that their disease will return in a worse form.

The Pharisees were not satisfied. They challenged Him to give them a sign about which there could be no mistake. He repudiated the suggestion with scorn. A sign that would compel belief would have no value at all. The only sign they would be granted would be that of Jonah. He was a sign to the Ninevites of approaching destruction. The people of Nineveh were wise in their generation and repented. Let the Pharisees do the same.

This business of 'signs' was a real difficulty and still is. We shall deal with it at length in a later chapter. We have already seen the rules laid down for Himself by Jesus at the outset of His ministry during the Temptation. But His contemporaries found His reticence on the subject hard to understand. Even the evangelist Matthew seems to have mixed up the 'sign of Jonah' with a symbolic parallel between the prophet's three nights in the belly of the 'whale' and Jesus' three days' burial in the tomb.

The document Q adds to this incident our Lord's freely expressed opinion of the Pharisees and Lawyers (or scribes). The occasion seems to have occurred when a Pharisee invited Him to a meal and then complained that He did not practise the usual ablution before eating.[1] To this Jesus replied that the Pharisees' care for external appearances was at complete variance with their lack of

[1] Lk. 11$^{37\text{ff}}$ cf. Mt. 23, Mk. 7, 12^{38}.

moral scruple. He proceeds to pronounce a number of 'Woes' against them which give detailed examples of this failing. When the lawyers complain that He seems to include them in this condemnation He utters further Woes against them, accusing them of failing to pursue the true ends of religious knowledge themselves, and of doing all in their power to hinder others from making the attempt. After this the Pharisees did everything they could to force Him into utterances that might discredit Him with the authorities, while Jesus on His part warned the people to avoid the taint of Pharisaism, which, He said, was hypocrisy.

Difficulties of another kind arose when certain of His hearers so far mistook the nature of Jesus' mission as to wish to make Him a referee in legal disputes. One such asked Him to order his brother to make proper division of their patrimony.[1] Jesus refused the role of arbitrator and turned the issue into one of real spiritual import by telling the story of the Rich Fool and so revealing the folly of covetousness. No one, says Jesus, knows when his last hour will come. It is therefore only sensible to be always prepared for the end and not to be completely immersed in the affairs of this life. When Peter asks Him whether this applies to His own disciples he is told that everyone should be faithful in the discharge of his duties. Those whose special business it is to help prepare for the coming of the Kingdom must not assume that they can afford to neglect commonplace affairs. They must remember that it is by their faithfulness in the daily task that their fitness for higher responsibilities will be judged.[2]

They are not to think that this was likely to be easy. It should already be clear that He Himself was not going to be universally accepted. Inevitably then His mission would

[1] Lk. 12^{13ff}.   [2] Mt. 24^{43ff}, Lk. 12^{39ff}.

give rise to greater dissensions still. The differences would manifest themselves in the very bosom of families. His would-be followers might even have to choose between Him and their own parents. There would be no escape from the necessity for decision. The signs that a great crisis was at hand should be obvious to all. People who boast that they can forecast the weather ought to be able to read the portents of the times. So they should make their preparations. Any sensible man who was threatened with a lawsuit would try to come to terms with his opponent before he became involved in the tedious and often venal processes of the law. In the same spirit everyone should make haste to see that he escape the danger of an unfavourable verdict before the judgment-seat of God.

This warning was reinforced when some members of the crowd told Him of an incident that had just happened in the Temple Courts. Pilate had actually caused the massacre of some Galileans while they were engaged upon their sacrifices.[1] We cannot place this incident, although we know that it is the kind of thing that did happen. It was paralleled by an attack upon some Samaritans on Mt. Gerizim which, according to Josephus, led to Pilate's ultimate recall. Jesus says that no one could suppose that these Galileans suffered such a fate because they were specially wicked, any more than those eighteen others were who were suddenly killed by the fall of a tower in Siloam. (This latter disaster was probably caused by Pilate's effort to improve the water-supply.) Anyone who wished to insure himself against such a sudden and unprepared end must undergo a change of heart. Crisis and death will certainly come, we must always be ready.

[1] Lk. 13^{1ff}.

II. FEAST OF DEDICATION

The scene changes to Jerusalem. It is winter and the Feast of the Dedication or Encaenia (Chanuka—renewal) is being observed. This festival had been instituted by Judas Maccabeus to commemorate the deliverance of the Temple from the defilements of Antiochus Epiphanes in December B.C. 165. During the festival Jesus was walking in Solomon's Cloister in the Temple and teaching there under cover because of the wintry weather.[1] The Jews surrounded Him, determined to get a definite answer to their insistent question whether He were really the Messiah or not. This, however, was not a question that admitted of a plain answer without fear of misunderstanding. Jesus had given them many means of coming to a conclusion for themselves. All that He will add now is that the work that He had already done as representing His Father should serve as a sufficient credential. Anyhow His questioners did not belong to His flock; if they did they would have understood all this quite easily, and they would certainly have been able to recognise that He was truly revealing His Father.

This stung the Jews to open resentment. They even fetched stones and made as if to stone Him. Jesus interrupted them: 'I have done many good deeds in your midst: for which of them are you going to stone Me?' 'For none of them, but for the blasphemy that leads you to claim divinity for yourself.' Jesus retorted with a quotation from the 82nd Psalm, in which Jehovah is represented as speaking to the judges, 'I said, "Ye are Gods".' If the sacred Scriptures could speak of human beings in that way He surely should not be stoned for

[1] Jn. 10$^{22\text{ff}}$.

using the same language. It was of course an *argumentum ad hominem*, but as such it was effective, and the immediate danger passed.

However, that did not prevent them from forming plans to arrest Him in a more legal fashion. He saw what was afoot and escaped by leaving Jerusalem and making His way to the eastern side of Jordan.[1] There He settled down for a time in the place where John had been accustomed to baptise. Many of the Baptist's sympathisers were still in the neighbourhood. It was natural that they should welcome Jesus, particularly as John had spoken of Him. They remembered that John had performed no miracles, yet they were prepared to accept his witness as true. All the more reason for them to accept Jesus, whose words were supported by many wonderful deeds. In this favourable environment Jesus remained some time and won many converts.

While He was in Perea He was asked about the success of His mission: 'Are there many being saved?'[2] As so often happened, Jesus gave an answer that seemed evasive. Entrance to the Kingdom is hard and the gate narrow. Many people would think a physical acquaintance with Messiah enough to ensure their admittance. But that is far from being true. The test for membership of the Kingdom is a moral one. Even the old Psalm had said (6^8), 'Depart from me, all ye workers of iniquity.' Many Jews would find themselves rejected on that score and representatives of the Gentiles occupying their places. Even blood-relationship to the Messiah is not enough for salvation.

At this time some of the Pharisees came to warn Him to leave.[3] Perea was part of the territory of Herod

[1] Mt. $19^{1\text{ff}}$, Mk. $10^{1\text{ff}}$, Jn. $10^{39\text{ff}}$.
[2] Lk. $13^{22\text{ff}}$.   [3] Lk. $13^{31\text{ff}}$.

Antipas, and Herod was planning to kill him, as he had already killed John the Baptist. 'That fox!' said Jesus, 'tell him that I shall continue My work so long as it is Mine to do. However, I shall have to be on My way soon to Jerusalem. No prophet can perish outside that city! It has always rejected and stoned God's messengers. I would have protected its people as a hen spreads her wings over her chicks. Now they must remain desolate. Yet I know that when I next enter its gates there will be those who will cry, "Blessed is He that cometh in the name of the Lord".'

Sometimes this anguished note in Jesus' utterances was replaced by one of sheer playfulness. At this time He was invited by a Pharisee to a meal[1] on the Sabbath day. A dropsical patient was present and Jesus challenged His hosts, knowing how carefully they watched Him, to say whether it was lawful to heal on the Sabbath or not. When they could not reply, He said, 'You would have done as much for a beast of burden if you had found it struggling in a ditch on the Sabbath.' And then in the awkward silence that followed He drew attention to the way in which people were scrambling for the best seats. 'That is all wrong, you know. If you want to make sure of a good seat you should always take one below your proper order of precedence. Then the host will be bound to notice it and call out to you "Here my dear fellow, you must come up higher." In any case if a host wants to give a banquet, of course he won't invite just those people who can ask him back again, but he will ask the poor and needy and wait for his reward in Heaven.'

'Happy,' said a fellow-guest, 'the man who sits down at the Messianic feast.' 'Yes, but it won't be all the

[1] Lk. 14:1ff.

invited who will sit down. People sometimes offer excuses for failing to turn up at a banquet. One must inspect a piece of property, another must test a couple of new draught animals, and a third has got married. No doubt that will happen at the Messianic banquet. You can't be surprised if the Host at *that* feast fetches in all the poor creatures who never get a square meal.'

Crowds would listen to this kind of teaching.[1] Jesus brought it home to them by saying that if they really wished to enjoy the advantages of the Kingdom they must make up their minds to put first things first. To follow Him they must be prepared if necessary even to desert their homes and to surrender life itself. They must count the cost beforehand, just like a land-owner about to build a watch-tower or a king about to start a war. You can't abandon such enterprises in the middle!

The Pharisees could still not get over the fact that He frequented the company of tax-collectors and other people outside the pale. To silence them Jesus told His most famous series of parables.[2] A man who has a hundred sheep and loses one will go hunting everywhere in the wildest places for the missing one. A woman who has lost one of the coins from her head-band, her wedding-ring, as we should say, will be in agonies and will turn the house upside down till she find it. Much greater will be the agony of the man whose son has left him and is known to have fallen into evil courses. All his wealth and the respectability of the remainder of his family will fail to satisfy him until the wanderer returns. In each of these cases there will be tremendous joy over the recovery of what is lost. But to the last of the three parables Jesus added an appendix to show that in the case of the supposedly virtuous there might be an

[1] Lk. 14^{25ff}.   [2] Lk. 15.

utter lack of this natural emotion. The prodigal's return was not welcomed by the elder brother, who sulked in jealousy because his own virtues seemed to be inadequately rewarded. The story had a universal application, but it was an especial rebuke to the religious section of the nation who could not bear to see the 'sinners' saved, and to the nation as a whole for its jealousy of the Gentiles.

III. RETURN TO JERUSALEM

Having thus revisited the scene of His earliest ministry and done what He could to 'prepare a people for Himself', Jesus felt that the time had come for Him to return to Jerusalem and put the issue to the final test. He had avoided arrest so far, but He was unlikely to do so much longer, and it was best to meet the challenge on ground of His own choosing. It was now Spring again, the Passover was approaching and Jerusalem during that feast afforded the best platform for any Jew who had a word from God to deliver to his nation.

The immediate occasion of His return to Judea was the sickness of Lazarus. Already on an earlier journey Jesus had been entertained at the house of Martha and Mary at Bethany. There He had occasion to notice the difference between the characters of the two sisters, one such a typical housewife, busy and practical, while the other was of the affectionate and contemplative type, happy to be in the presence of those she loved, but inclined to be neglectful of practical details and creaturely comforts. Both were devoted to Him in their respective ways, and when their brother Lazarus fell sick they sent into Perea to tell Him.[1] Jesus did not seem to make

[1] Jn. 11$^{1\text{ff}}$.

much of it, merely remarking that the illness was not likely to prove fatal. The disciples were all the more surprised when a couple of days later He said they would go to Judea. They remonstrated, pointing out the danger. Jesus, however, told them that Lazarus was dead. Seeing His determination, Thomas said they might as well go and face their fate with Him.

The whole world knows the subsequent story of the raising of Lazarus, told with incomparable simplicity and artistry by the author of the Fourth Gospel. The event produced a double reaction. Many of the witnesses accepted the claim of Jesus to be the Messiah. Others took the news to the Pharisees. It immediately led to an impromptu gathering of the Sanhedrin. The members were in a quandary. They recognised that Jesus was gaining a wide reputation as a wonder-worker, but they were afraid that this might lead to a popular rising and that it might bring down upon them the wrath of their Roman masters. Their discussion was interrupted by Caiaphas who was the High Priest in that fateful year.[1] It was stupid, he said, not to recognise that it would be much better for one man to be put to death rather than for the whole nation to be destroyed, thus uttering an unwitting prophecy of Jesus' atoning sacrifice. The pronouncement decided the policy of the Sanhedrin. From that moment they began to lay their plans to accomplish His destruction, and even issued orders that anyone who knew His whereabouts should inform them. For the time being, therefore, Jesus avoided Jerusalem and withdrew to the thinly populated region immediately to the north, where lay the village of Ephraim.

In the meantime the crowds were beginning to

[1] By Jewish law the office was held for life, but the Romans changed the occupant at will. Caiaphas held it from A.D. 18 to 36.

THE PERIOD OF OPPOSITION

assemble in Jerusalem, so that they could complete their ceremonial purification before the feast began.[1] There was a good deal of speculation about Jesus. He was not to be found anywhere and people began to wonder whether He would appear at all during the feast.

Actually He was already making His way back from Ephraim through Jericho towards Jerusalem. He was filled with a solemn feeling of exaltation, and the disciples, seeing how withdrawn He was, could not shake off a heavy foreboding.[2] Presently He called the Twelve to Him and proceeded to give them a very clear idea of what He expected to happen in Jerusalem. Indignities would be heaped upon Him and He would be crucified, but that would not be the end, for death would not be able to hold Him.[3] In spite of the apparent clarity of this prediction and in spite of all His earlier warnings, they could make nothing of it. His doom was indeed difficult enough to believe in, for it would mean the end of all the hopes they had learnt from Him.

Even now there were compensating incidents. At Jericho the chief local customs officer, Zacchaeus, made a notable effort to see Him.[4] A small man, he knew he would stand no chance in the crowd; so he climbed up into a fig-mulberry. Jesus saw him and aroused the wrath of the nationalists by craving his hospitality. But Zacchaeus showed his sincerity by pledging himself to make voluntary restitution to all whom he had defrauded and to hand over half his wealth to the poor. As Jesus left the town He was accosted by a blind man,[5] Bartimaeus, who refused to be silenced by the crowd but

---

[1] Jn. 11^{55}.   [2] Mk. 10^{32}.
[3] Mt. 20^{17ff}, Mk. 10^{32ff}, Lk. 18^{31ff}.   [4] Lk. 19^{1ff}.
[5] Mt. 20^{30ff}, Mk. 10^{48ff}, Lk. 18^{35ff}. (Two, according to Matthew).

insisted on attracting Jesus' attention. Jesus was moved by the man's persistence, a sure sign of faith, and sent for him and healed him.

We next hear of Jesus at Bethany where Lazarus was, whom He had raised from the dead.[1] This was the Saturday six days before the Passover was due. He was invited to the house of Simon, a wealthy man, who had suffered from leprosy. Lazarus was a fellow-guest and his sisters were also there. Martha, as usual, was helping with the household chores. Mary, again in character, gave expression to her affection in what seemed to the company a most extravagant way, using a very costly perfume to refresh the head and feet of Jesus and going so far as to use her own hair in place of a towel. Jesus accepted the act because He recognised the passion of love that had prompted it. But it brought out the latent antagonism of one of His own disciples, Judas Iscariot, who, repelled by what he had seen, set to work to plot His betrayal.

This brings us to the last week of Christ's earthly life. But before we enter upon the story of the Passion we must look back to consider the meaning of the Lord's miracles.

[1] Jn. $12^{1\text{ff}}$.

CHAPTER X

THE WONDER-WORKER

I. THE STORIES ESSENTIAL TO THE NARRATIVE

THE most casual reader of the gospels must be aware that a large part of the narrative is taken up with stories of the wonderful deeds done by Jesus. It is true that some modern scholars have tried to belittle the amount of space given to these accounts, while others have suggested that they are tales told by professional story-tellers and have no essential relation to the documents in which they have been incorporated. These efforts to rid oneself of what is felt to be an inconvenient element in a biography are unworthy of serious historians.

There is no denying the amount of space devoted to the subject. In Mark the stories occupy just about a third of the whole book. Moreover they are to be found not only in Mark but in all the documents from which the gospels are built up. It is impossible to find a memoir of Christ which does not incorporate them. Nor can we dismiss them as mere legends spun by some travelling story-teller about a national hero and having no value except the intrinsic fascination of the narrative itself. There is too serious a purpose about them, which lifts them out of the class of sub-historic folk-lore. They fit too closely into the texture of the whole narration. They form too obvious an element in the thought of Jesus Himself. We shall be well advised if we begin by taking the stories as they stand and trying to look at the events with the eyes of the chief actor in them.

II. THE MOTIVE OF COMPASSION

It is clear that Jesus, being what He was, must have rejoiced in the opportunity of bringing health and succour to the afflicted. When He saw the multitudes and remembered that they had been long without food, He 'had compassion on them' and set about meeting their need. Similarly He had compassion on the Widow of Nain and restored to her her son. He had compassion on the two blind men and gave them their sight (Mt. 20^{34}). Coming off the boat He had compassion on the crowds and healed their sick (14^{14}). He told the demoniac to let his friends know that his cure was due to the Lord's compassion (Mk. 5^{19}). But there is no need to multiply examples. It would be impossible to eliminate the motive of compassion from Jesus' wonderful works, although some modern commentators seem disposed to make the attempt, because they have recognised an even more powerful motive.

It is suggested that pity cannot have been a sufficient impulse since there were comparatively few who could be healed. This sounds rather like the excuse of a government department which will not allow a few to receive a benefit that cannot be open to all. But our dislike of it should not blind us to the fact that there was indeed another and perhaps even stronger motive for these wonderful works. They were intended to show that the Kingdom of God had come.

This does not mean that they were intended to compel people's belief in the coming of the Kingdom. We have already seen that Jesus refused to use His gift in such a way. In any case He was as ready as His contemporaries to recognise that other religious leaders could perform wonderful works and even perhaps that the Devil himself could inspire a capacity for exorcism. 'If I by Beelzebub cast out devils, by whom do your sons cast them out?' (Mt. 12^{27}).

By the same token the miracles were not intended as proofs of His divinity, for He tells His disciples to do the same things (Mt. 10^8). Such deeds were not regarded as beyond the capacity of humanity. If they were not demanded as the universal accompaniments of religious authority (no one claimed them in the case of John the Baptist), they were at least accepted as natural in the case of an inspired teacher, and the Pharisees could with some show of reason demand a special sign to substantiate what they understood to be Jesus' special claim.

There was however one event in connection with which such signs were very generally expected, and that was the coming of the Messianic Kingdom. So Jesus Himself instructed the disciples of John to tell their master that they had seen such wonders as should remove all doubts (Mt. 11$^{2\,\text{ff.}}$). So also in His sermon in the synagogue at Nazareth, having read the passage from Isaiah, 'He has sent me to proclaim release to the captives and recovering of sight to the blind,' Jesus exclaimed. 'Today this scripture has been fulfilled in your hearing' (Lk. 4^{21}). The wonderful works were evidence that the long-promised power had appeared on the earth. That power could be experienced by those who knew themselves to be members of the Kingdom. When the disciples were unable to heal the epileptic boy, it was because they had forgotten that they were within this new covenant, and they were rebuked for their lack of faith (Mt. 17^{20}, Mk. 9$^{28-29}$). The wonders of Jesus were signs that spoke from faith to faith. Where there was no faith there were no miracles. They belonged to the Kingdom. Only within that environment had they meaning. To those who had eyes to see and ears to hear they witnessed to the greatness, the power and the goodness of God (Mk. 8[18], Lk. 10[23]). So when the Twelve were sent out on their mission to proclaim the Kingdom of God it was natural that they should be told also to heal the sick and the mentally distressed (Mk. 6[7], Mt. 10[1], Lk. 9[1]).

III. TERMS EMPLOYED

This interpretation is borne out by a consideration of the various terms used to designate these acts. Sometimes they are called just *erga*, works, a neutral word suggesting that they are the characteristic deeds of Jesus. A more significant word is *terata*, wonders or portents. This emphasises the marvellous element, but suggests a hidden meaning. *Dynameis*, mighty works or more literally 'powers', indicates the force or ability displayed in the act. Finally there is the term *semeia*, signs, which most definitely brings out the fact that the acts are not ends in themselves, but are intended to point to something beyond themselves. As we should naturally expect from the character of the Fourth Gospel, this last is the word most commonly used there. The whole collection of words makes it clear that these events ought not to be considered in isolation as mere facts. If it is always true that 'there is no fact without value', it is specially true in this instance that we shall never penetrate to the true inwardness of the events unless we try to understand them in relation to their whole context. They belong not only to the realm of history, but also to that of theology.

Further light is thrown on this aspect of the case when we consider the varied character of the acts themselves.

The simplest of them to our modern notions are the acts of healing. If a century or two ago it seemed to require a special effort of faith to accept them, no such effort is required today. We know so much about the influence of mind over body that we are quite prepared to recognise that even organic disease can often yield to suggestion. Cases of demoniacal possession are now generally, though not always, explained as nervous disorders, and they notoriously yield to the impact of a powerful personality. If Jesus Himself accepted the common belief of His time in the activity of malevolent spirits, that would probably increase rather than diminish His power to heal.

The bringing of the dead back to life raises a more difficult question, although there have been modern instances in which a heart that has ceased to beat has been made to function again. But here we have to be particularly careful not to read into the narrative more than the writer intended to convey. It is possible that we sometimes assume death where the New Testament writer has at least left the question open. The case of Lazarus is in a different category. There can be no doubt that the writer of the Fourth Gospel, to whom alone we owe this instance, repeatedly emphasises the evidence of death. The doubt arises in the minds of some modern scholars whether he intends the narrative to be taken as a purely factual record or as allegory. The use of allegory would be in accord with the well-known method of the 'spiritual' gospel, but there is no other example of it on this scale, and it is probably wise not to assume allegory unless the intention to use it is unmistakable.

The same caution in the interpretation of the gospel narrative should be observed in the case of what are known as the 'nature' miracles, the stilling of the storm, the conversion of water into wine, the feeding of the multitudes and so on. While, however, we must not make the event appear more unusual than it is intended to be, we must not be too ready to accept a rationalising explanation. Often such explanations are ludicrously out of keeping with the context and are so puerile as to amount to an inverted superstition. The best rule is to take the narrative at its face value, unless there are clear indications to the contrary.

IV. CREDIBILITY

In estimating the credibility of any particular 'sign' we shall thus form as exact a judgment as possible of the evidence. But beyond the actual evidence we shall of necessity pay heed to the way in which the narrative fits in with the whole context of revelation. Is it congruous with all that we know of the character of Christ, and of the coming of the Kingdom? Is it suitable as an element in God's revelation of Himself? This is of particular importance in regard to the raising of the dead and to the 'nature' miracles. But it is of quite fundamental importance in regard to the two greatest 'signs' of all, the Incarnation and the Resurrection. Here it is specially obvious that no material evidence could be sufficient to 'prove' the facts. The evidence may give us some ground for belief, but in the last resort we shall only accept it if we think it likely that 'God would act like that'. Certainly there can be no doubt as to the necessity of these events to the very existence of Christianity as we know it. Without the Incarnation there would have been no Resurrection, and without the Resurrection there would have been no Church, no Bible, no Creed, no Sacraments, no Ministry—unless indeed one could think that all these things could be built up on a mere hallucination. And that would be the greatest miracle of all.

One objection we seldom have to meet today, and that is the blank denial of those who say that 'miracles cannot happen'. As Augustine said long ago miracles are 'not contrary to nature, but contrary to what we know of nature'. Or as a modern writer has said, 'A miracle in the biblical sense is an event which happens in a manner contrary to the regularly observed processes of nature.'[1] As we have seen, our capacity for the exact observation of nature has grown enormously with succeeding generations, and we have now little difficulty in accepting as true many events which seemed quite inexplicable even to our grandparents. It is possible that events which are inexplicable to us may become equally capable of explanation to our grandchildren. In any case materialistic determinism no longer seems a necessary philosophy to a science that believes itself to have discovered an element of indeterminism in the very constitution of matter. To the Christian the observed 'laws' of nature are the expression of the will of God and there appears no reason why God should not apply those laws from time to time in a special manner to suit His purposes. As His fixed purpose is the salvation of man there would be nothing capricious in such action. We cannot sum up the discussion in words wiser than those of Professor Joad, 'If God created the world and is or may be immanent in it, it might be expected that He would from time to time intervene in its affairs. In fact He intervenes continuously, if only through the instrument of grace by means of which He works upon us. But it is also on this assumption quite reasonable to

[1] A. Richardson, *Theological Word Book*, p. 152. S.C.M.

expect certain special interferences such as Christianity, with its record of the series of God's mighty acts, affirms.'[1]

In estimating any 'miracle' story we should therefore ask the following questions:

1. What exactly does the narrator say?
2. Is his story meant to be taken literally or allegorically?
3. What evidence is there in other New Testament documents or elsewhere to support his account?
4. Is any 'natural' explanation of the event possible?
5. Does the event, if inexplicable by known natural law, fit in with what we know as the 'scheme of salvation'?

The answers to these questions will help us to distinguish sharply between the general sobriety of the New Testament and the exuberance of the Apocryphal Gospels. They will also reveal that some of the New Testament 'wonders' are much more strongly attested than others, so that in some instances we must suspend judgment. They may even help us to decide how far we should be justified in making the act of faith necessary to accept as factually true events which cannot be 'proved' by the natural reason alone. We may be further helped if we remind ourselves that in the last resort all religion demands an act of faith. The existence neither of God nor of the soul is susceptible of mathematical or 'scientific' demonstration. Nor indeed are such universally accepted realities as goodness and beauty.

[1] C. E. M. Joad, *Recovery of Belief*, pp. 232-3. Faber and Faber.

CHAPTER XI

THE PASSION

THE narrative of the last few days of our Lord's earthly life takes up proportionately quite the largest share of the Gospel story. That it should do so is no doubt evidence of the great importance attached to the redeeming work of Christ and especially to what became known in later days as the Atonement. It may also be due to the fact that an account of the Passion was separately compiled and was widely circulated before our Gospels took their present shape. For the first time in dealing with the life of Jesus Christ we are able, in spite of some minor discrepancies in the documents, to compile a day to day diary of events.

SUNDAY

On the morning after the meal at the house of Simon the Leper, Jesus determined to make His entry into Jerusalem. This was to be done publicly and significantly. There could no longer be any secrecy, although He would not give any unnecessary handle to His opponents. When He and His party reached Bethphage on the Mount of Olives He sent two of His disciples into a neighbouring village,[1] telling them to bring back a donkey's foal which they would find tethered there, and which the owner would be quite ready to let Him have. We can feel the atmosphere in which these events occur. 'The Evangelist thinks of the whole episode as having

[1] Mt. 21$^{1\text{ff}}$, Mk. 11$^{1\text{ff}}$, Lk. 19$^{29\text{ff}}$, Jn. 12$^{12\text{ff}}$.

been designed and arranged by Jesus in accordance with His insight into the purposes of God. The ass was provided and ready, as He knew that it would be; He foresaw that the protests of its owners would at once be abandoned when His message was given; and the ass was, as it happened, an animal meet for the service required of it, since it was a colt, *whereon no man ever yet sat.*'[1] There is no need to postulate any miraculous prevision. The whole story may well move on the plane of the natural. 'The accounts of the Passion in the Synoptic Gospels clearly imply that our Lord already possesses staunch friends both in Jerusalem and in the villages on the slopes of Mt. Olivet, as well as determined enemies in the city itself.'

If the fact that Jesus rides into Jerusalem shows that He will publicly accept the role of Messiah, the fact that He rides on an ass and not on a horse shows that He will come 'lowly' and not as a conquering warrior. It is still the ideal of the Suffering Servant and not that of the popular Davidic King that He exemplifies. The disciples and the populace do not yet understand the difference. Their palms and Hosannas hail the forceful Deliverer coming to claim His people's freedom. The Pharisees feared the consequences of the demonstration. 'Control your disciples.' But things have gone too far for that. 'If I silenced them, the very stones would cry out.'

As they descended the hill, at a turn in the road the 'cloud-capped towers, gorgeous palaces' of Jerusalem leapt into view. The sudden vision moved Jesus to tears. He sees in prospect the religious capital of His people robbed of its majesty and beauty, its buildings razed to the ground, its citizens put to the sword. And

[1] Rawlinson, *The Gospel according to St. Mark*, pp. 151, 152. Methuen.

all this because they could not distinguish the true source of peace. Entering the city He found everything in an uproar and all the new-comers asking who He was. His own people gave the safest answer, 'Jesus the prophet from Nazareth in Galilee.' They claimed Him as a 'holy man' and said no word about a king.

Arrived in the city Jesus made it His business, like every good pilgrim, to pay a visit to the Temple. He took careful note of all that was going on, and returned in the evening with the Twelve to Bethany.

MONDAY

The next day Jesus and His disciples returned to Jerusalem. On the way occurred the incident of the Barren Fig-Tree.[1] This is a puzzle to modern commentators. If we take it literally it seems like an exhibition of unreasoning bad temper. No one would expect to find figs before June, nor would anyone try to eat the green knops which are the promise of ultimate fruit. On the other hand we cannot just dismiss the story because it is difficult. There is one possible explanation. It had been the prophetic tradition in Israel to drive a lesson home by the use of some striking symbolic action. It was part of the 'visual aids' in religious education. Our Lord was on this occasion acting in accordance with His prophetic role. The 'cursing' of the fig-tree was as symbolic as the triumphal entry into Jerusalem. Few things can look more refreshing than a fig-tree in full leaf. In this case it was mere show, particularly if the leaves when parted disclosed no knops. It was a just picture of contemporary Judaism. The destruction of the one portrayed the fate of the other.

[1] Mt. 21^{18ff}, Mk. 11^{12ff}.

134 THE LIFE OF JESUS CHRIST

An even more highly dramatic and symbolic action was witnessed when Jesus made His way to the Temple. He found, as He knew from His inspection the day before that He would find, the courts of the building filled with a crowd of traffickers dealing in the multifarious goods needed in the Temple worship. There were dealers in the birds and animals to be sacrificed, and there were money changers, who provided in exchange for the Roman currency in secular use the Syrian half-shekel, in which the Temple tax had to be paid. All these Jesus drove out of the sacred precincts, and at the same time He stopped the porters from using the courts as a short cut from one part of the town to another.

Some commentators have seen in this action a practical demonstration of opposition to the whole custom of animal sacrifice. There is, however, no evidence for this. No doubt the practice of Christianity would ultimately put an end to such sacrifices, and in any case they did of necessity cease when the Temple was destroyed in A.D. 70. Our Lord, however, seems to have regarded the system as valid at least for the time. It is notorious both that He paid the Temple tax Himself and that His followers continued to share in the Temple worship after He Himself had been crucified. We must conclude that He never spoke against animal sacrifices. Certainly no such word has been recorded. They had been a part of God's early education of His people. What He was concerned about was the chicanery and the downright dishonesty with which the traffic was carried on. 'My house,' He quoted, 'shall be called a house of prayer, but you have made it a den of robbers.'[1]

Certainly the action was intended to have a significance

[1] Mt. $21^{12\text{ff}}$, Mk. $11^{15\text{ff}}$, Lk. $19^{45\text{ff}}$, Jn. 2^{13}.

wider than its immediate effect. It was symbolic of the cleansing of the whole religion of Judaism from those evil elements of which He had so often complained. Even in 'fulfilling' the Law He had gone much further than that reform movement which had been inaugurated by John the Baptist. He had provided new bottles for His own new wine. The Fourth Gospel heightens this symbolic interest by putting the incident at the beginning of His ministry and by telling how He improvised a whip to make His action the more effective. The modern reader is helped to realise the outstanding personal dominance of this Teacher who, for all His gentleness, could in a moment of supreme indignation cut through generations of abuse and subdue a hostile crowd to His will.

The rest of the day Jesus spent in the now quiet Temple busy with His customary tasks of teaching and healing. A delightful touch was added to the scene, when some of the children, engaged in various duties about the Temple, recognised the Teacher whom they had seen welcomed to the city the previous day, and began to chant in His honour the song they had then heard, 'Hosanna to the Son of David'. This was more than the authorities could bear. 'Don't you hear what they are shouting?' 'Yes, but haven't you ever read that out of the mouths of babes and sucklings God would perfect praise?' The officials looked for an opportunity to bring about His destruction, but at the moment there was nothing they could do; the crowd was too thick about Him and too engrossed in His words.

TUESDAY

That night Jesus spent again in Bethany. On the Tuesday morning as they returned to the city the disciples drew His attention to the fig-tree, which was now completely withered.[1] He took the opportunity to speak to them on the necessity of faith. If they had sufficient faith they could do greater wonders than this, and could indeed remove whole mountains of difficulty. The right attitude, if they wanted anything in accordance with God's will, was to believe that in the providence of God they already had it, and they would find their prayers fulfilled. If they wished to cultivate that spirit they must be very careful not to harbour a grudge against anyone. Love and faith together are the surest index to right and fruitful action.

On arrival at the Temple He strolled through the courts, busy in discussion. He was soon interrupted by the religious leaders who wanted to know what was His authority for the things He was doing.[2] No doubt they had specially in mind His cleansing of the Temple, but they also questioned His authority as a teacher. He retorted with another question. John the Baptist, where did he get his authority? That question they dared not answer. If they had said that he had received their own formal commission, the crowd would have resented it because they knew very well that John was not one of the recognised official teachers, but believed him to have spoken by direct inspiration like the old prophets. If on the other hand they had agreed and said that he was God-inspired, the *riposte* would have been, 'Then why did you not support him and join in his reform?' Therefore they refused to answer and Jesus also was relieved of the necessity to answer. But the obvious inference was that His authority too, like John's, was from above.

This attack from the Temple officers opened the way

[1] (Mt. 21$^{20\text{ff}}$), Mk. 11^{20}. [2] Mt. 21$^{23\text{ff}}$, Mk. 11$^{27\text{ff}}$, Lk. 20$^{1\text{ff}}$.

THE PASSION 137

for similar attempts by other representative bodies. The first were the Herodians, the court party.[1] They wanted to know whether He agreed with the paying of taxes. They hoped that if He did agree they might embroil Him with the nationalist Jews, while if He did not He might become equally embroiled with the Roman authorities. The payment of the head-tax was still a burning question. It had been imposed by the Romans first in A.D. 6 and had led to a serious revolt by Judas the Gaulonite (Acts 5^{37}). Although the revolt had been crushed, feeling still ran high. It was even too high for the Rabbis themselves, for it was one of their maxims that a governor must be held legal ruler of any district in which his currency held good, and his head stamped upon a coin marked it as his own. Jesus escaped from this dilemma by sending for a *denarius*. 'Whose head is this?' 'Tiberius Caesar's.' 'Then pay to Caesar what is Caesar's and to God what is God's.' The contrast no doubt is between the *denarius* that is paid to the Roman Government and the half-shekel that is paid to the Temple. But the saying is capable of very wide application and has set the standard of Christian attitude to the State for many centuries.

The Sadduccees came next with a kind of Hyde Park question about the future life.[2] According to the Levirate law (Deut. 25^{5-10}), if a man had married and died childless, it was the duty of his brother to take the widow in order that the dead man might still have an heir. In this way, they alleged, a woman had had seven successive husbands. Which one was to claim her in the life beyond the grave? The question was not quite so silly as it seems to us, because such contemporary

[1] Mt. $22^{15\text{ff}}$, Mk. $12^{13\text{ff}}$, Lk. $20^{20\text{ff}}$.
[2] Mt. $22^{23\text{ff}}$, Mk. $12^{18\text{ff}}$, Lk. $20^{27\text{ff}}$.

Jews as had achieved belief in a resurrection were inclined to think of the next life as a close replica of this. Jesus' answer makes it clear that physical conditions do not prevail in the other world and so the question has no meaning. But he also takes the opportunity to affirm the doctrine of a future life, basing it upon the indissoluble nature of our association with God.

Last came the Pharisees. They put forward one of their own number who was a trained lawyer or scribe.[1] He asks a stock question, 'Which is the great commandment in the Law?' The Rabbis reckoned that in the Law there were 613 commandments, either negative or positive. Some argued the question which were the most important, while others deprecated such argument altogether. Jesus cut through the argument by quoting the summary of the Law, which was probably quite well known, and so drawing out the two fundamental principles of love to God and to one's neighbour. The lawyer immediately conceded the point and volunteered the further view that this was more important than all the ceremonial provisions of the Law. Jesus was so pleased with this honest and clear-sighted response that He told the lawyer that he almost qualified for membership in the Messianic Kingdom. On this note the whole discussion ended and Jesus was bothered with no more questions.

Tuesday in Holy Week is sometimes called the Day of Questions, but the questioning did not occupy the whole day. A number of other recorded events suggest that this was one of the most crowded days in the Lord's life. He found time to give a good deal of concerted teaching while He was still in the Temple. The three parables, of the Two Sons, of the Wicked Husbandmen

[1] Mt. 22³⁴ff, Mk. 12²⁸ff.

THE PASSION

and of the Wedding Feast,[1] are all assigned to this occasion. So also is the warning against the example of the scribes and Pharisees in Mt. 23[1-10]. It is true, said Jesus, that they sit in Moses' Seat, that is that they occupy the position of authority.[2] Therefore their instructions must be obeyed. But their personal character is not to be taken as a pattern. They carry big text-boxes, or phylacteries, on their foreheads, and wear long tassels to their robes, and they are very pompous in their love of titles and orders of precedence. In contrast with them, members of the Kingdom must reckon themselves as all on the same level of value under Christ.

Actually a remarkable contrast to the ostentatious display of the scribes and Pharisees was observed by Jesus as He sat near the alms-boxes.[3] These articles were trumpet-shaped, and important people dropping in heavy coins could make them resound very loudly as their contributions clattered down the narrow necks. But Jesus saw a poor widow drop in two mites, which together did not make up more than a farthing and were so light as to make no sound at all. However, they were all she had, and she did not even keep one back to buy herself a morsel of bread. She, said Jesus, in the sight of God had contributed more than all the rest. True giving is sacrificial giving.

One specially illuminating event occurred before Jesus left the Temple.[4] Philip and Andrew told Him that certain Greeks (who had probably become proselytes and were therefore admitted to the Court of the Gentiles)

[1] Mt. 21[28]–22[14].
[2] Moses' Seat was an actual throne in the synagogue, apparently occupied by the presiding elder, with the seats of the other elders to right and left of him.
[3] Mk. 12[41ff].
[4] Jn. 12[20-50].

had expressed a desire to see Him. It was to Philip that the request had been made, and he was perhaps a little embarrassed by it, as there had been no suggestion that Gentiles should be included in their missionary activities. However, he had consulted Andrew, and the latter, with his usual skill in helping people out of difficulties, brought him to Jesus. We can have little doubt that Jesus granted an interview to the foreigners. In any case He saw in the request evidence of the future success of His work, and it fortified Him as He thought of His approaching end. 'A grain of wheat must lose its own life if it is to produce other grains. One must not cling to life. If any man joins Me he will share My fate, but he will also share My honour.' While Jesus was talking in this strain there was a sound of thunder, which some bystanders, as their forefathers had so often done,[1] interpreted as the voice of God, the Bath-Qol, which had been heard already at His Baptism and Transfiguration. Jesus, like Socrates and Joan of Arc and many other completely devoted natures, believed that God spoke immediately to Him, and now He heard in the thunder a message of direct reassurance for Himself. God had before in history made clear His own power and majesty, and He would do so again.

As they were leaving the Temple one of His disciples drew Jesus' attention to the immense stones that were being used in the reconstruction of the building.[2] This work had been started by Herod the Great in B.C. 20 and was intended by him to be the greatest achievement of his life. No doubt he hoped by it to conciliate Jewish opinion which had always been contemptuous of him as a foreigner, an Idumean or Edomite. The plans were

[1] Ex. 9^{28}, 2 Sam. 22^{14}, Ps. 29^3, Job 37^5, Jer. 10^{13}.
[2] Mt. 24^1, Mk. 13^1, Lk. 21^5.

so grandiose that the work had taken much longer than was expected. It was not actually completed till A.D. 64. Six years later it was all to be destroyed in the terrible siege of Jerusalem. Jesus foresaw some such catastrophe and did not hesitate to say so. To Jews this would sound the most terrible blasphemy. The Temple was the visible expression of God's presence among them, and to prophesy its destruction seemed almost like declaring the approaching end of God. Some commentators hold that it was on this ground that Jesus was finally condemned.

At the moment Jesus used the incident as an introduction to a particularly solemn discourse about events that might be expected in the future. As they were returning to Bethany, he took four of His disciples, Peter, James, John and Andrew, out on to the slopes of Olivet, and while they sat and looked back over the city, He began to talk to them about the coming catastrophe.

What follows is given in the form of an Apocalypse, a type of prophecy with which our Lord, of course, was perfectly familiar. It was characterised by three distinct traits. First it used figures and symbols which, while being sufficiently clear to those for whom it was intended, would conceal its meaning from the uninitiated. It is possible that 'the Abomination of Desolation' is such a figure in the present passage.[1] Second, in the exhaustion of all human aid, it represents the only chance of salvation as lying in God's personal intervention. Third, it foreshortens the future, allowing little or no interval between the present and the end. As in a

[1] Mk. 13^{14}, Mt. 24^{15}. The phrase comes from Dan. 9^{27} where it probably refers to the heathen altar of Zeus set up by Antiochus Epiphanes in the Temple on the site of the altar of burnt offering. (See also 1 Macc. 1^{54}.)

cinema the picture thrown upon the screen presents us with a flat surface without any stereoscopic effects, so in apocalyptic literature there are no long vistas; the immediate and the final are inextricably mixed.

It is generally agreed that in this apocalyptic discourse the other two synoptists have based their accounts on that of St. Mark. Matthew has modified it so as to give more attention to the 'consummation of the age'. In Mark the disciples merely ask when the destruction of the Temple will take place, while in Matthew they ask also, 'What will be the sign of Thy Parousia?' Luke on the other hand emphasises the safety of the disciples in the midst of the catastrophe ('not a hair of your head shall perish'), and he replaces the cryptic reference to the 'abomination of desolation' with a picture of Jerusalem surrounded with armies. The explanation of these changes probably lies in the fact that, whereas Mark was published before the fall of Jerusalem, Matthew and Luke were almost certainly composed after it. This event was so shattering a cataclysm that it must have made a great difference to every writer. It involved the end of the Jews for many centuries as a separate nation and involved profound changes in Judaism as a religion. Such changes were bound to be reflected in any literature of the period.

A more searching question is how far we can regard the Marcan account itself as an original utterance of our Lord. Some scholars have accepted it as so completely representing the mind of Christ that all the rest of His teaching is to be interpreted in the light of it. He was, they think, a typical apocalyptist consumed by the idea of the immediacy of the end, unique only in that He saw Himself as its principal agent. Other scholars, however, say it is so unlike the rest of Christ's teaching

THE PASSION

that it must really be in origin nothing more or less than a distinctively Jewish apocalypse, into which some authentic sayings of Christ have been inserted. Neither alternative is necessary. It is much more natural and more nearly consonant with the facts as a whole to regard it as representing a genuine discourse of Jesus. Here He is deliberately adopting the style of the apocalypses. His disciples, familiar with the style, would know how to interpret it. They would recognise that what He was trying to instil into them was complete confidence in God's providence. If they had the same difficulty as we experience in disentangling references to the destruction of the Temple from references to the end of the age, they would know that He made no profession of knowing the exact dates which the Father had kept in His own power, and they would see in the destruction of Jerusalem at least a stage in the coming of the Kingdom.

In any case the practical duty before them was to be continually on the watch. They must not allow themselves to be taken by surprise as had the generations of Noah and Lot. They would never know precisely when God's call would come. They must always be listening for it. This practical lesson was reinforced by three great parables, the Ten Virgins, the Talents, and the Sheep and the Goats.

WEDNESDAY

After the exhausting efforts of the previous day Jesus seems to have spent the Wednesday quietly in Bethany.[1] We know very little of what happened on this day. Some harmonists would like to insert here the incident of the woman taken in adultery,[2] but others regard this incident,

[1] Lk. 21$^{37\text{ff}}$.   [2] Jn. 8$^{2\text{ff}}$.

since it has no very good manuscript authority, as being a mere piece of apocrypha. Some with a greater degree of probability would put on this day the meal at the house of Simon the Leper, which we have taken as belonging to the Saturday before Palm Sunday. To take it on the Wednesday, with its reference to Judas' impatience at what he took to be Jesus' complacent acceptance of Mary's extravagance, would at least fit in well with his apparently sudden determination to betray Him.

What we do know is that this day Jesus warned His disciples of the nearness of His doom. As far as He Himself was concerned the end was already determined. 'It is only two days now to the Passover. It is then that I shall be given up to be crucified.'[1]

In fact a meeting was even then being held at which plans were laid for His destruction. Caiaphas had called together some of the leaders and they tried to think of some charge on which He could be tried and executed.[2] However, they came to the conclusion that it would be unsafe to attempt such a scheme during the feast while Jerusalem was so full of Christ's friends from the country. They were on the point of giving up the idea for the present when an unexpected opportunity arose through the defection of Judas.

What put it into the mind of Judas of Kerioth to betray his Master is not clear. It has been suggested that he did it in order to force Jesus' hand and make Him declare Himself openly as the Messianic King. But the reference to Judas' misappropriation of the company's money suggests that he was not the kind of man to stake everything on an outburst of patriotism. The probability is that he was not only disappointed in

[1] Mt. 26^1, Jn. 13^1.   [2] Mt. 26^{3ff}, Mk. 14^{1ff}, Lk. 22^{1ff}.

his Messianic hopes—Jesus' apparent lack of interest in practical ways and means would be sufficient cause for that—but that he was also prompted by a sordid desire for gain. He was quite prepared to serve his Master as long as there was any hope of getting something out of Him, but when that hope failed he could still make something out of betraying Him to the authorities. He went to the officers of the Temple guard and asked them what reward they would offer. The chief priests said thirty silver pieces, about £5, the statutory price of a slave. For that he agreed to lead them to Jesus at the first favourable opportunity when He was not surrounded by the usual crowds.

CHAPTER XII

THE LAST DAYS

MAUNDY THURSDAY

THE following day Jesus began to make arrangements for the keeping of the Passover. As leader of His band of disciples He would act in regard to them as a kind of house-father, and He would preside at their meals, particularly at those that had a religious character. No doubt they had been accustomed often to dine with each other at such a *haburah* or fellowship meal. There is some doubt whether the meal for which Jesus now made preparation was a *Qiddush* or sacred meal as a prelude to the Passover, or whether it was the Passover itself. This doubt is reflected in our documents. Mark, and indeed all three synoptists, appear to think of it as the Passover.[1] John, however, is quite clear that Jesus was crucified at the very time that the Passover lamb was slain, and that the meal now in question took place on the night before. In this instance, although scholarly opinion is not unanimous, the majority verdict seems to be in favour of John's presentation as against Mark's. Even if the meal was not the Passover and was therefore not subject to the ritual regulations of the feast, it would, nevertheless, occurring on the eve, have some proleptic associations of the whole period of 'unleavened bread'. Since Jesus foresaw that it would be His last meal with

---

[1] It is true that all the messengers are told to do is to *prepare*, but the assumption appears to be that the meal will be eaten the same evening and that it will be the Passover (Mk. 14$^{16-17}$).

THE LAST DAYS

His disciples the preparations for it would be undertaken with unusual care.

He tells Peter and John to go into the city and make the necessary arrangements. They will know the house Jesus has chosen because they will see a man carrying a pitcher of water, and all they have to do is to follow him. The man performing this task will be easily distinguishable because as a rule it was the women of the household who fetched the water from the well. Jesus evidently knew the house and its family. He is quite sure that the owner will grant them hospitality. Any householder would be expected to offer such facilities at the Passover, but the attractive suggestion has been made that in this case the host was the father of Mark and therefore well-known to the circle of Jesus. The evangelists, looking back in later days, felt that all these events had been predestined, and in the narrative each detail, however small, is invested with an air of special solemnity and significance. All happened as Jesus said. The disciples prepared the meal in the large upstairs room placed at their disposal.[1]

In the evening they all took their places at the table, and at once it was apparent that Jesus regarded this as a very special occasion. To their astonishment He equipped Himself like a household slave with a towel and, taking a basin of water, began to go round washing their feet.[2] Peter objected to this menial service being performed by their Master, 'Thou shalt never wash my feet.' Jesus insisted. 'If you do not accept this office at My hands you will show that you do not share either My work or My character.' 'Then,' said Peter with his usual impetuosity, 'not my feet only, but also my hands and my head.' Jesus curbed his exuberance. If a man

[1] Mt. 26^{17ff}, Mk. 14^{12ff}, Lk. 22^{7ff}. [2] Jn. 13^{3ff}.

before going out to dine has had his bath, and then walks in his open-work sandals through the dusty streets, he needs only the washing of his feet and then is clean 'every whit'. The whole action was highly symbolical. It may have contained some suggestion that a man who has once been converted to faith in Christ and has experienced in baptism the full forgiveness of his sins, needs only penitence to cleanse him from the occasional defilements he contracts on life's journey. The lesson Jesus Himself read into it was that of complete humility in the service of others, a service that must be rendered by all to all, irrespective of rank or position. It was a prelude to the utterance of that great New Commandment of universal love which was the basis of the whole Christian ethic, and was to give the name Maundy (*mandatum*) to the day on which it was pronounced.

So they were clean. But not all. Jesus was oppressed with the thought that one of those present was ready to betray Him. He began to warn the company what was to happen. They found the warning scarcely credible. Who would do such a thing? Peter motioned to John, who was reclining next to Jesus, to find out who it was. Jesus replied that it was the one to whom He would present the piece of bread when He had dipped it in the common dish. But this was so ordinary an act of Eastern courtesy that no one noticed when He passed it to Judas of Kerioth. The latter, however, understood its significance; and when Jesus told him to get on with what he had to do, he slipped out to warn the Temple guards to be ready. The rest made nothing of it, thinking that Judas, as the keeper of their funds, had merely been told to make some necessary purchases for the coming feast.

When Judas had gone Jesus set about one of the

customary rites of such occasions, the pronouncing of a blessing by the presiding member over bread and wine. According to the fixed formula this took the shape of a blessing of God for the gifts of food and drink, very much as our 'grace' before and after meat does today. But the additional words used by Jesus on this occasion were quite unprecedented and must have come as a great surprise to the disciples, who would be expecting no more than the usual form. What He was about to do He invested with a special degree of solemnity by telling them[1] that He had desired ardently to eat the Passover with them, but that now He would not be able to do so until it gave place to the Messianic banquet in the Kingdom of God. This eschatological reference was to be reaffirmed later on.

He then took the round, flat *chapattie* or loaf of bread,[2] pronounced the customary blessing, broke it and handed it to His disciples. As He did so He said, 'Take this and eat it. It is My body, which is given for you. Do it as a memorial of Me.' What meaning this astonishing announcement had for the disciples at that moment we do not know. They must at least have taken it as referring to His imminent death, of which He had forewarned them, and they may have recognised that death as a sacrifice to be made on their behalf. But the idea of eating His body, even if it were only in symbol, must have seemed extremely strange. If they had time to reflect they may possibly have realised the implied suggestion of the most intimate possible union with Him, or even of the assimilation of His personality by them.

During the meal several cups of wine were passed

[1] Lk. 22^{15}.
[2] Mt. 26^{26ff}, Mk. 14^{22ff}, Lk. 22^{19ff}, 1 Cor. 11^{23ff}.

round. Jesus took one of them and said over it the customary formula of blessing. 'All of you drink it,' He added, 'this cup is My blood of the new covenant which is being poured out for you and for many others for the remission of sins. Do this every time you drink it, as a memorial of Me.' This would be even more surprising. To Jews blood meant one thing and one thing only. It was the vital energy, the 'life', whether of animal or man, and to taste it was strictly forbidden. Indeed all their elaborate laws for the slaughtering of animals were intended to secure that the blood should never reach human lips. To be told now to drink something that Jesus called His 'blood' would be as surprising to them as a hint of cannibalism would be to us. More understandable to the disciples would be the reference to the new covenant. Jesus was saying that He was inaugurating a new dispensation—this was the dividing of the ways—and as the first covenant had been sealed with blood of animals, so the second should be sealed with His blood. Those who drank it would be entering into the new dispensation. Again this is given an eschatological reference. It was an anticipation of the banquet in the Kingdom of Heaven. 'I will not drink wine again till I drink with you the new wine at the Messianic banquet in the Kingdom of God.' Or as St. Paul puts it, 'As often as you eat this Bread and drink this Cup you show forth the Lord's death till He come.'

After this Jesus spoke long to His disciples, not explaining these things directly, but drawing out the spiritual realities that lay behind them. John devotes no fewer than four chapters to these discourses.[1] He can do so, because he has taken the institution of the

[1] Jn. 14–17.

Eucharist for granted and given no space to it. In any case he has dealt much earlier, in chapter VI, with its significance. Now he shows how Jesus tried to comfort His disciples, promising to send His Spirit to take His place in their hearts, showing how He is united to them as closely as the vine to its branches, so that the same essential life flows through both, warning them of future persecution, and concluding with the great High Priestly prayer, in which He discloses in the form of a thanksgiving addressed to God His mediatorial relationship between His Father and His followers.

When this was over they joined in singing the Hallel (Ps. 113-18) and went out as usual to the Mount of Olives. On the way Jesus warned them that they would soon be parted from Him and that they would betray Him.[1] Peter of course hotly asserted the impossibility of any such thing, but Jesus gave him a special warning of his own approaching defection. He went on to remind them of the old days when He sent them out alone. 'Did you find yourselves sufficiently equipped?' 'Quite sufficiently.' 'But now,' He said, 'you will need all the equipment you can get, even swords.' They took Him literally. 'Well, here are two swords.' 'That is enough of that,' He said, and broke off the conversation.

While they were talking they had crossed the brook Kidron and had come to the olive plantation of Gethsemane, a place to which they had often resorted and which was well known to Judas.[2] There Jesus left the majority of the disciples to rest but took with Him the favourite three, Peter, James and John, to a more retired spot. He invited them to keep watch with Him while He went to pray in solitude. The immediate

[1] Mt. 26^{30ff}, Mk. 14^{26ff}, Lk. 22^{31ff}.
[2] Mt. 26^{36ff}, Mk. 14^{32ff}, Lk. 22^{40ff}.

prospect of the coming trial overwhelmed Him, and in great agony of spirit He prayed that He might be spared the ordeal. Yet if it is God's will He will accept it. After an interval He comes back seeking relief in the companionship of His three disciples, but finds them asleep. Three times is this experience repeated. He has to bear His mental anguish alone except for the spiritual ministration He receives from heaven. Someone later recorded that the sweat poured from Him in such quantities as to seem like drops of blood falling to the ground. At last the struggle was ended. He was convinced that His hour was come and that He must go to meet it. He aroused the sleeping apostles, and, conscious now of the approach of armed men, bade them accompany Him.

Judas had led a detachment of the Temple police, armed with swords and clubs, to the spot, and arranged that he should mark down their man for them by greeting Him with a kiss, the usual salutation for a Rabbi. To avoid possibility of mistake he does it with exaggerated fervour, and earns the rebuke from Jesus, 'Do you betray Me with a kiss?' Without waiting for an answer Jesus asked the guard whom they wanted, and when they replied 'Jesus of Nazareth' He acknowledged that He was Himself the man. They were so cowed that the question and answer had to be repeated before they dared arrest Him.

That was the signal for the two disciples who were still carrying their swords in case of trouble. One of them, Peter, impetuous as ever, made for a serving man belonging to the High Priest and slashed off his right ear. Jesus told him to put up his sword and immediately attended to the wounded man. He then turned to the crowd and made a dignified protest against the manner of His arrest. 'Why should you attack Me like this as if I were a bandit? You could have found Me at any time teaching in the Temple and could have taken Me quite easily.' When the disciples saw that He was giving Himself up they scattered and fled. Only one young man, probably Mark, followed the posse as it moved off in the darkness. But when one of the band detected him and caught hold of his wrap, he twisted out of the garment and made good his escape.

The soldiers bound Jesus for greater security and led Him off to Annas, who had been High Priest before his son-in-law Caiaphas, and had probably taken a leading part in the plan for His arrest. He interrogated Jesus about His followers and His teaching. It is probable that his purpose was to decide the nature of the charges that could best be brought against the prisoner. Jesus answered that everything He had done was open and there was no need for such questioning. One of the officers struck Jesus for His alleged impertinence, but the examination was closed and further awkward questions about His followers were avoided.

Annas wasted no further time, but sent Jesus, as in duty bound, to Caiaphas, the reigning High Priest. He summoned a hasty and informal meeting of the Sanhedrin. The members arrived as soon as it was light and began to examine their prisoner. They asked Him whether He was the Messiah. When He returned an evasive answer they brought forward professional informers, who said that He had threatened to destroy the Temple; but the witnesses did not agree about the details and their evidence was useless. Caiaphas took the examination in hand himself, and challenged Jesus to say whether He really was the true Messiah or no. Jesus then answered plainly: 'I am; and one day you shall see

Me seated on God's throne and returning in the clouds of Heaven.' This was enough. The High Priest tore his vestments as a sign of horror and proclaimed Him a blasphemer. The Council unanimously agreed that He should be put to death and the soldiers began to mock and insult Him.

In the meantime Peter was in difficulties and suffered a severe blow to his pride. He and another disciple, probably John, had pulled themselves together sufficiently to catch up with the soldiers and their prisoner. When they arrived at the High Priest's palace his companion, who had some acquaintance with the High Priest, spoke to the concierge and they were allowed in. During the examination Peter sat by the brazier of coals in the courtyard. Several of the servants, men and women, thought they recognised him, but twice Peter's vehement denials silenced their suspicions. At last he was challenged by a relative of Malchus, the soldier whose ear he had cut off in Gethsemane. Others joined in and professed to identify him by his Galilean accent. By this time Peter was thoroughly frightened. He added blustering curses to his denials, and convinced his tormentors that he was no follower of Christ. But in the silence he heard a cock crowing. He turned instinctively as he remembered his Master's words, 'Before the cock crow twice thou shalt deny Me thrice.' He saw Jesus gazing down at him, and he rushed out into the night weeping bitter tears.

Judas was in worse case.[1] When he knew the result of the examination he saw what he had done and was filled with remorse. He brought back to the chief priests the money they had given him and tried to put it into the Temple treasury. They would not let it be

---

[1] Mt. 27³ff, Acts 1¹⁸ff.

used for sacred purposes because it was 'the price of blood'. Either he or they bought with it a piece of land which was known afterwards as the Field of Blood, and was used as a burial-place for foreigners. Matthew tells us that Judas committed suicide by hanging, Luke that he 'burst asunder in the midst'. There have been instances in which the latter fate has accompanied hanging, and this may have been one of them.

Although the Sanhedrin had condemned Jesus to death they had to get the Roman authorities to corroborate and carry out the sentence. While, therefore, it was still early in the morning they sent Jesus to Pilate the Procurator.[1] They could not enter the governor's palace or they would have become 'defiled' and would have been prevented from sharing in the Passover meal. Pilate, respecting their scruple, came out to them and asked what was the charge against the prisoner. It was no good preferring against Him in this court the charge of blasphemy on which they themselves had condemned Him. They tried more appropriate tactics. 'Of inciting the nation to rebellion. He advised them not to pay the poll-tax and said that He Himself was a King, the Messiah.' This was a charge that Pilate could not ignore. He took Jesus and personally examined Him. When he found that the only Kingship Christ claimed was of a moral and spiritual order he told the Jews that he could find no substance in their charges. They continued, however, to reiterate them, and Pilate was at a loss when Jesus made no effort to answer. Someone mentioned that Jesus had come from Galilee. Pilate immediately jumped at the opportunity to be polite to Herod Antipas who at that time was in Jerusalem, and also to escape responsibility. The latter hope was

[1] Mt. 27^{1ff}, Lk. 23^{1ff}, Jn. 18^{28ff}.

disappointed. Antipas could draw no answer from Jesus to his interrogation. All he could do was to let his soldiers make brutal sport of the prisoner and then send Him back to the Procurator.

The duty of decision thus rested squarely on Pilate, but the situation was ugly and he did not wish to precipitate an outbreak of violence. He tried persuasive measures. Neither he nor Herod had been able to find any crime in the man: would they not be satisfied with the indignities He had already suffered and let Him go? In any case he was accustomed to release some condemned prisoner annually at this festival: would they not let Jesus take advantage of this amnesty? But the suggestion aroused the fury of the crowd. They did not want this man released, but Barabbas, a notorious bandit, a convicted fomenter of sedition against the Romans but withal a popular hero.

Pilate felt constrained to let them have their choice. He made, however, one appeal to their compassion. He let the soldiers take Jesus away and subject Him to their cruel sense of sport. When they had finished with Him they dressed Him up again in the mock royal insignia, and Pilate led Him out to the people. 'Behold the man.' But they only cried 'Crucify Him'. Pilate was now hesitating between the superstitious fears engendered by his wife's recital of a dream she had had about his prisoner, and the more tangible warning of the Jews, that if he let the prisoner go he would be acting as a traitor to Caesar. In the end he tried again to escape responsibility by a pitiable exhibition of indecision. He called for water and 'washed his hands' of the whole business. In doing so, like most undecided people, he had given the case away. To his everlasting disgrace the fact remained that he released Barabbas and 'delivered Jesus to their will'.

GOOD FRIDAY

The soldiers stripped the mocking robes from Jesus and replaced them with His own clothes. Two other prisoners, both of them bandits, were to be executed at the same time and they were all led off together. Each, according to the custom, was carrying his own cross. Jesus, exhausted by the long agony of the night with its repeated scourgings and the five distinct trials through which He had had to go, sank under His load.[1] The guard impressed a foreigner from Cyrene, named Simon, to carry the cross for Him. A great crowd followed, and there were many, particularly among the women, who openly mourned for Him in the noisy manner of the East. Jesus bade them not to weep for Him, but for the unhappy fate that would descend upon the rising generation.[2]

It was about nine o'clock when they reached the hill Golgotha outside the gate of the city, which was the place for the execution. There they offered the prisoners a narcotic to deaden their nerves before the pain began, but Jesus refused it. The three prisoners were then fastened to their respective crosses and raised aloft to die a most agonising and lingering death. Each had his charge, written in the three current languages, nailed to his cross so that all might read the reason for his execution. Pilate had offended the Jews by making Jesus' charge read, 'This is Jesus of Nazareth the King of the Jews.' Each had four guards who were responsible for his execution. The clothes of the prisoners were the perquisites of these soldiers. Beneath the cross of Jesus His guards were tossing dice to share out His garments. Each soldier got a separate article of clothing, but that

[1] Mt. $27^{32\text{ff}}$, Mk. 15^{21}, Lk. 23^{26}, Jn. 19^{17}. [2] Lk. 23^{27-28}.

left the long cassock-like inner coat still unalloted. To this there were no seams, and to have divided it would have ruined it; so the soldiers tossed to see who should have it whole. Jesus looked out upon this scene and upon the gloating religious leaders and the jeering passers-by. Surging waves of pity broke over Him and He kept crying out, 'Father, forgive them for they know not what they do.'[1]

Extraordinary as it may seem, one of His fellow-sufferers began to seek relief from his own pain by joining in the mockery. The other was of a very different mould. Knowing that Jesus was no bandit like themselves, and recognising from His demeanour that He had been unjustly condemned, he had come to believe in the truth of that claim which they were all deriding. He accepted Him as Messiah and asked to be admitted into the Messianic Kingdom. 'Lord, remember me when Thou comest into Thy Kingdom.' Jesus took this seriously and answered it with equal seriousness. 'Today shalt thou be with Me in Paradise.'[2] Mary, the Mother of Jesus, together with John and a few of the faithful women, had found her way to the foot of the Cross. Jesus did not wish her to remain during the terror of His deepest agony. He committed her to John's keeping, 'Mother, behold thy son. Son, behold thy mother.'[3] John seems immediately to have taken her away and from that time to have given her a home with himself.

Jesus' worst hours coincided with an obscuration of the sun. From noon till about three there was general darkness which was paralleled by the blackness in His soul. He suffered from a profound sense of dereliction. Even in Gethsemane He had been conscious of heavenly ministrations, but now He had no conscious feeling of

[1] Lk. 23³⁴.   [2] Lk. 23³⁹⁻⁴³.   [3] Jn. 19²⁵ff.

THE LAST DAYS 159

the Presence of God. As the spasm passed and He came out of the mental agony, the words of a familiar hymn fell from His lips, 'My God, My God, why didst Thou forsake Me?'[1] (Ps. 22[1]). Psychological exhaustion added to the physical strain made Him cry out for relief, 'I am thirsty.'[2] One of the bystanders dipped a sponge in the sour wine of the country and putting it on a soldier's javelin, touched it to His lips. Jesus drank gratefully, knowing that all was now over. Thus momentarily strengthened He cried out triumphantly, 'It is finished.'[3] And then with His last sigh He repeated the prayer which all Jewish boys said every evening of their life, 'Father, into Thy hands I commend My spirit',[4] another quotation from a much loved hymn (Ps. 31[5]).

The synoptists tell us that at this moment there was a great portent in the Temple. The immense veil that divided the Holy Place from the inner sanctuary, or Holy of Holies, which was only opened once a year for the High Priest to perform the rites of the Day of Atonement, was rent from top to bottom.[5] As the author of the Epistle to the Hebrews was later to show, this was symbolic of the opening, through the death of Christ, of the way into most intimate communion with God for all believers. Matthew, who accumulates such incidents, tells us that there was also a great earthquake, that many graves were burst open and that the bodies of a number of saints emerged, and were actually seen in the city. This is a point at which the canonical record approaches the spirit of the apocryphal gospels.

When the officer and the guard on Golgotha saw that Jesus had died, and took note of the darkness and of

[1] Mk. 15$^{33-34}$.   [2] Jn. 19$^{28-29}$.   [3] Jn. 19^{30}.
[4] Lk. 23^{46}.   [5] Mt. 27$^{51\text{ff}}$, Mk. 15^{38}, Lk. 23^{45}.

the earthquake, they were thoroughly frightened. 'This was an innocent man,' they said, 'He was a son of God.'

It was the soldiers' duty to remain on watch until the prisoners were all dead. The Jews began to get restive as the day drew on, for presently the Passover would have to be eaten and it was contrary to the Mosaic law to have bodies thus exposed during the feast. They asked whether death could not be hastened by breaking the prisoners' legs. The soldiers agreed, and did as was asked in the case of the two bandits, using the heavy mallet that was kept for the purpose. When they came to Jesus they knew that He was already dead, but to make assurance doubly sure a soldier thrust his spear into His side.[1] It was especially noted, as being unusual in the case of a dead body, that blood and water flowed from the wound. What is the explanation medical men are not agreed. There can be little doubt why John so carefully recorded it. He was writing against people who professed to believe that Jesus was no actual person of flesh and blood, but a phantom. Blood and water were generally regarded as the fundamental elements of which the human body was composed. The fact that they were exuded on this occasion showed that the Lord's body was real.

That same body was given honourable burial. One of Jesus' secret disciples, Joseph of Arimathea, who was also a member of the Sanhedrin, summoned up enough courage to ask Pilate to allow him to take charge of the corpse. Assisted by Nicodemus, another secret disciple, he took the body down, wrapped it with a considerable weight of spices in a clean shroud and buried it, in a garden hard by, in a new tomb which he had just had

[1] Jn. 19$^{31\text{ff}}$.

THE LAST DAYS 161

excavated for himself, cut out of the living rock. From a distance they were watched by several of the women followers of Jesus. When they saw Joseph roll the great stone to close the entrance to the tomb they knew that everything was as secure as it could be, and they left to prepare further spices and ointments, realising that nothing further could be done until the next day, the Sabbath,[1] had passed.

SATURDAY

Of what happened on that Sabbath we have very little knowledge. As it was the rest day there could be no activity. Some scholars think that the disciples dispersed immediately for their home in Galilee, but the law against travelling on the Sabbath would make that impossible. Certainly the despair induced by what they felt to be irreparable disaster must have paralysed their energies. All their hopes were disappointed, and they were uncertain whether or no they would have to share the fate of their Master. It is most likely that they went to earth in the back streets of Jerusalem.

The 'chief priests and Pharisees' did not wish to leave anything to chance. They remembered Jesus' repeated assurances that He would rise again, and although they attached no more importance to such predictions than did the disciples at that moment, they thought it possible that His followers might make away with the body and then claim that His prediction had been fulfilled. They sought an interview with the Procurator and put the situation as they saw it to him.[2] He recognised the force of the argument and told them gruffly to take a guard from among his own soldiers and make the thing safe.

[1] Mt. 27^{60ff}, Mk. 15^{46ff}, Lk. 23^{53ff}. [2] Mt. 27^{62ff}.

They not only set the guard but sealed the entrance stone.

That is the story of the Pharisees' action as Matthew alone narrates it. He must have got it from his own special source. We can imagine with what care he preserved and recorded it in view of what was to happen later.

CHAPTER XIII

THE TRIUMPH

1. THE RESURRECTION

WE have come to the end of the earthly life of Jesus Christ, and there, if we had been attempting it, ordinary historical writing would also end. But we have not professed to be engaged upon a merely historical task. We have never concealed from ourselves the fact that there was more here than science or history can grasp. We have been conscious that from the moment, not only of the birth, but of the conception, of Jesus there were spiritual forces at work which could not be caught within the net of pedestrian criticism.

Even if we had been writing a merely human biography and the events of Holy Week had been the end, we should still not have written off the life as a failure. No doubt the disciples in the first heaviness of their loss felt it as such. We with our better opportunity for reflection can see in it a great triumph, of good over evil, of human frailty over imperial power, of faith and love over religious prejudice. It is the triumph of the hero who freely surrenders his life in the attempt to save his fellows.

It is not, however, for that reason that the evangelists give so large a space to the events of that week. They have something more to record, and it is in the addendum to their narrative that they find a new and rich explanation of all that has gone before. They have indeed given hints of it all the way through. They have shown how

Jesus Himself tried to prepare the way for this explanation, and they have been accurate enough to reveal how dull and slow were the disciples to grasp what the Lord was so carefully trying to make clear to them. Now they themselves have to record what it was that gave the note of real and ultimate triumph to the message of salvation. Jesus was declared to be the Son of God with power. Death, which had seized Him, could not hold Him. He rose again.

Here we must remember that, as in the case of the wonderful birth, we are at one of those moments when the vertical line of eternity strikes most conspicuously across the horizontal line of time. We cannot carry our historical methods into eternity, we can only record what is seen and known and experienced within the sphere of time. But happily at this point our historical evidence is multiplied. We have not only the statements of the four evangelists with the oral teaching and the documents on which they rest, but also the detailed evidence of St. Paul, who wrote before any of them. To this we must add the belief of all the other New Testament writers. Indeed this whole library of books was written from the point of view of the Resurrection, and would be almost meaningless without it. After that, of course, we get the evidence of the Fathers which broadens out into the total witness of the age-long Church of Christ. Here we shall be content to follow the method we have pursued hitherto, and rely upon the documents as we have them.

II. THE WOMEN AT THE TOMB

It was before sunrise on the Sunday morning that Mary Magdalene and the other women went with their

THE TRIUMPH 165

spices to the sepulchre. As they went they discussed anxiously who would roll away for them the great stone that sealed the entrance of the tomb. They did not know that during the night there had been another earthquake tremor during which the stone had actually been displaced. This had terrified the guards, who had seen an apparition of an angel like lightning seated upon the stone which he had rolled away.[1]

When the women came to the tomb they were astonished to find it not only open but empty. While they were wondering what had happened two men in glittering white appeared to them and told them that Jesus had risen, reminding them of His own words on the subject. The women ran off at once to tell the Eleven and the others. Mary Magdalene found Peter and John and told them that the body of Jesus had disappeared. The two hurried off at once to see for themselves. John, who was the younger, got there a little ahead and stooped to look in. He saw the shroud still there, but before he could make up his mind what had happened he was thrust aside by Peter, who went right in and saw not only the shroud but also the head napkin neatly folded, lying by itself. They had to believe the evidence of their own eyes, but what it meant they could not tell.

In the meantime Mary Magdalene had returned to the tomb and remained disconsolate in the garden. Suddenly she heard someone asking her why she was weeping. Thinking it was the gardener she asked him what he had done with the body. The voice said 'Mary' and at once she recognised it as that of Jesus Himself, and swinging round she exclaimed, 'Rabboni, my Master!' By this time the other women were also

[1] Mt. 28$^{1\text{ff}}$, Cf. Mk. 16$^{1\text{ff}}$, Lk. 24$^{1\text{ff}}$, Jn. 20$^{1\text{ff}}$.

back, and recognising Him, they all fell down and clung to His feet. 'Don't cling to Me,' He said, 'but let My disciples know that later I will see them in Galilee.' They went immediately to tell the disciples, but they could not make them believe their story.

While this was going on the guards had reported the loss of the body to the chief priests. They hastily summoned a meeting and formed a plan to give a natural explanation for the disappearance. They bribed the guards to say that while they were asleep the disciples had come and stolen the body. At the same time they promised that if the tale came to the ears of the Procurator they would do their best to see that the soldiers came to no harm. The story thus invented long held currency among the Jews.

III. TWO DISCIPLES AT EMMAUS

That evening two of Jesus' followers were walking out of Jerusalem towards Emmaus,[1] a village on the road to Joppa. They were naturally talking about all that had been happening and trying to make sense of the curious stories about the empty tomb. A stranger caught up with them and joined in their conversation. He proved to be well read in the Scriptures and expressed surprise that they had not expected the Messiah to suffer an ignominious death, and then to rise again. They were so enthralled by this exposition of the Scriptures that when they arrived at the village they invited him to go in with them and share their meal. After the usual Eastern gesture of unwillingness and the consequent polite pressure, he consented. At the meal he surprised

[1] Lk. 24^{13}.

them by acting as the host and breaking the bread in a way which revealed to them that he was none other than Jesus Himself. As soon as they recognised Him, He vanished, and they rushed straight back to Jerusalem with the good news of His Resurrection. They found the disciples gathered behind locked doors for fear of the Jews. But their news was already old. Before they could get it out they were told that Jesus had indeed risen. Some time during the day He had appeared to Peter, and that was evidence which they must all accept.

While they were still recounting the story they were startled by the sudden appearance of Jesus in their midst. They thought at first that He was a disembodied spirit. He gently chided them for their fear, and pointed out that He still bore the imprint of His wounds. For further confirmation He asked for something to eat, and consumed a little fish before them all.[1] Jesus then proceeded to give the disciples their commission. 'Receive ye the Holy Spirit: whosoever sins ye forgive, they are forgiven unto them; whosoever sins ye retain, they are retained.'[2] Then they were at last convinced. All but one. Thomas was not with them at the time, and when he was told about it he said that he would never be able to bring himself to believe unless he could actually touch the mark of the wounds. The next Sunday evening the same thing occurred. This time Thomas was there, and Jesus told him to put out his hand and touch the wounds. Then at last Thomas could doubt no longer, but cried out 'My Lord and my God.' 'You have believed,' said Jesus, 'because you have seen Me. Happy are they who believe without such physical evidence.'

[1] Lk. 24$^{36\text{ff}}$. [2] Jn. 20^{26}.

IV. THIRD APPEARANCE TO DISCIPLES

The third appearance to the disciples as a body took place in Galilee. Peter and the other fishermen among them had decided to take up for a time their old occupation, and had gone out in the boats. After a fruitless night's work they were hailed in the dim dawn light by a figure from the shore asking if they had had any luck.[1] When they gave a negative answer, the stranger said 'Why not try on the other side of the boat?' Perhaps thinking the person standing at the higher level could see a shoal which was hidden from them, they did so, and this time they took so enormous a catch that they could not get the net in. John thereupon recognised the stranger as the Master. Peter immediately jumped overboard and began wading ashore, leaving the rest to tow the net in. They found that Jesus had a fire burning and had prepared them a breakfast of bread and fish.[2] When it was over Jesus put some questions to Peter, testing his love for Him, in spite of his denial at the trial. Three times He asked him whether he still loved Him. Peter was hurt by this repeated question, but he stuck to his statement of real affection. Then Jesus solemnly and in the presence of them all reinstated him and told him to take up his pastoral work for the flock of Christ. To this He added a warning of the martyrdom he would ultimately suffer. When Peter showed some curiosity as to the fate of John he was told that that was not his business: his duty was to follow his Master.

For forty days Jesus made occasional appearances to

[1] Jn. 21[1ff].
[2] An alternative suggestion is that He had prepared the meal for Himself and invited them to join Him.

His disciples. On one occasion[1] they were with Him on a mountain in Galilee. There were some who were still doubtful about Him. But He announced to them that He had now been given 'all power in Heaven and on earth'. It was their duty to persuade all the nations to accept Him. With this charge Matthew ends his gospel. He attributes to Jesus on that occasion not only the command to 'make disciples of all the nations', but also the instruction to baptise them in the threefold name of Father, Son and Holy Ghost.

St. Paul tells us of some of these appearances[2] and adds a mention of two which would otherwise have gone unrecorded, one to James (probably the Lord's brother who later took charge of the Church in Jerusalem), and the other to more than 500 of His followers, some of whom were still living when St. Paul wrote. Mark on the other hand does not give us independent information here. It is generally believed that his gospel has suffered some mutilation at this point. It seems likely that the genuine Marcan document ends at 16^8. In any case what follows, from 16^9 to the end of the book is probably a compilation from the other gospels and not an independent witness.

V. FINAL APPEARANCE

It is St. Luke who in his gospel and in the Acts tells us of the last appearance.[3] He omits the events in Galilee and we must suppose that the disciples had now returned to Jerusalem. There Jesus told them to wait until they 'received power' as the result of the promised gift of the Holy Spirit. They asked Him whether it would be long, and whether He would at that time

---
[1] Mt. 28^{16ff}. [2] 1 Cor. 15^{5ff}. [3] Lk. 24^{50ff}, Acts 1^{4ff}.

establish the full Messianic Kingdom in Israel. He told them not to worry about dates, which were after all in God's hands. All they were concerned with was their duty to act as faithful witnesses of all the things they had already experienced. They were to begin in Jerusalem, and spread the good news through Judea and then into Samaria, and so on till it reached the farthest corners of the earth. After those instructions He led them out on the way to Bethany to the old familiar spot on the Mount of Olives. He raised His hands in a gesture of blessing. As He did so He was separated from them and appeared to be raised from the earth. At this moment a cloud swept across the mountain and He was no more seen. While the disciples were looking after Him they became aware of two men in white robes, who told them that it was no use looking for Jesus; He had passed into another state of existence, but one day He would come again. The disciples recognised this to mean that the series of post-resurrection appearances was over. A new era had begun, the era of the Holy Spirit and the Church. They returned to Jerusalem and awaited the sign that was to set them to their task of preparing the way for the visible coming of the Kingdom of God.

CHAPTER XIV

THE FOUR PORTRAITS

IN the prevailing atmosphere of historical agnosticism when even the secular historians have such little confidence in their data, it is sometimes doubted whether we can be sufficiently sure of our facts to paint any worthwhile portrait of Christ. However, no one would deny that in the New Testament we actually have several portraits. Apart from the impressionist sketch given by St. Paul there are the four pictures drawn by the four evangelists, each of them no doubt affected by the needs of the particular clientèle for which it was composed, but all alike professing to be true likenesses of the same individual.

The question is whether they are really portraits of the same person. We have had many conflicting pictures in our own day, which on a superficial view have seemed so strongly contrasted as to be mutually contradictory. There is the 'gentle Jesus, meek and mild' of the children's hymns, flanked by the starry-eyed Galilean peasant of Rénan's *Vie de Jésus*. There is Harnack's ethical teacher, proclaiming the fatherhood of God and the brotherhood of man, challenged by Schweitzer's apocalyptic visionary believing that his own death will immediately usher in the final coming of God's Kingdom.

It must be admitted that the striking dissimilarity between these representations lends some justification to those who are uneasy about the more conventional portraits of Jesus. One is bound to ask whether the Christ the Church proclaims and worships can possibly have any relation to these unusual figures. The answer is that each succeeding presentation catches some one feature and exaggerates it at the expense of the rest until the resultant picture becomes a caricature rather than a genuine portrait. This is quite unlike what is to be found in the New Testament, where seemingly contradictory features are combined even by each separate artist, and yet the portraits are all quite obviously representative of the same subject. In all of them alike there is the man of humble position who is recognised as the Messiah and Son of God, who gives Himself to the task of saving His people from their sins, who teaches wonderful truths and does marvellous works, who is crucified but rises to a new state of existence from the dead.

I. INFLUENCE OF ST. PAUL

Of this figure St. Paul gives us his own individual outline. It is an impression rather than an outline, because St. Paul is not trying to present us with a portrait of Christ. That is not his task. He is trying to give us 'the mind of Christ'; and to do that he has to make no more than occasional and almost casual reference to incidents in the life of Jesus. To him the Christ was a universal being who existed before the worlds and 'emptied' Himself of His heavenly glory to become Jesus of Nazareth. As He was before the world, so He would be after it, handing over the sovereignty He had acquired into the hands of His Father at the end of this temporal age. During the short span of His earthly life He revealed Himself as the dictator of history. His purpose was to unite all men to each other and to God. This He did by uniting men to Himself. He broke down the barriers men had erected between Jew and Gentile and between themselves and

God. By faith and sacrament He incorporated believers into Himself. In Him they found themselves at one with God and each other; in that unity they could overcome death and enjoy the glory of eternal life.

It is easy enough to see how this picture agrees with the general, composite portrait we have already drawn from the New Testament as a whole. There can be no doubt that to St. Paul the cosmic Christ is identical with the Jesus of history. But it is not the same picture. It is sketched from a highly individual angle. That is not the same angle as is characteristic of any one of the four evangelists. This fact is specially interesting because Paul began writing already in A.D. 50, only twenty years or so after Jesus' crucifixion, and Mark, the earliest of the four gospels was written a decade and a half later, after Paul had ceased writing,

In view of Paul's vigour and genius you would have expected him to have influenced decisively the writings of men who came so soon after him. Indeed attempts have been made to explain nearly the whole of the evangelists' work as a kind of deutero-Paulinism, but the attempts have been widely regarded as failures and have now been generally abandoned. It adds much to the verisimilitude of the evangelists' writing that they took so individual a line. And it adds of course to the number of the witnesses we can count to the credit of the record.

II. THE MYSTERIOUS REDEEMER OF MARK

When we examine the Marcan gospel we feel entitled to ascribe an independent portrait to the writer because the account he gives us must be a selection deliberately made by him from the current tradition, if not from his own personal knowledge or from the testimony of some individual eye-witness such as St. Peter. In any case the author does not so much describe the actual appearance and character of Jesus as allow us to judge of both from the words and actions he records. The selection must have been made with the deliberate purpose of presenting a particular portrait. It has turned out to be of quite enormous importance, because it has affected not only the subsequent evangelists but the whole picture that Christians have held of their Lord ever since. This was the first full portrait, and it inevitably affected the rest.

Jesus as Mark sees Him is a mysterious figure, presenting a series of contrasts, which Mark's journalistic flair is quick to seize and express. He is at once human and supernatural. He reveals himself in acts rather than in words. It is questionable whether Mark had access to any collection of Jesus' sayings, such as the Q source used by the other synoptists, but if he had, he made little use of it. He left his subject to speak rather by example than by precept. There is a bluntness about the opening of his narrative which suggests a new Genesis. Compare 'In the beginning God', with 'The beginning of the gospel of Jesus Christ'. In one sentence Jesus comes 'out of the everywhere into here'.

After this summary announcement Mark plunges straight into his narrative and introduces his hero, just as He is about to start on His mission. There is no lingering over birth and childhood. The numinous character is suggested by the announcement of the fore-runner, himself a wild and strange figure with a background of the desert and intimations from prophecy. Jesus is ready to attach himself to the movement John has started. He is baptised and immediately experiences a divine communication assuring Him of His unique relation to God. The Spirit rests upon Him and on the instant impels Him into the wilderness, there no doubt to ponder the lines along which His mission will be conducted. He is tested by Satan, surrounded by wild beasts, and attended by angels.

John's arrest opens the way for Jesus' mission to begin. It has to be remembered that Mark was writing at a time when Nero's horrible persecution of the Christians was occupying the thoughts of all followers of the new religion far and near. Since Mark's gospel was probably written for a Roman congregation or one that had close affinities with Rome, it would be valuable at such a time to bring out clearly Jesus' courage and endurance under trial. We see how He steps at once into the shoes of the Baptist, iterates John's teaching on the imminence of the Kingdom, carries on his movement, and continues his unique type of baptism.

The decision thus to set about his mission had already been taken in the wilderness where, before beginning his active work, Jesus had met the chief enemy of mankind. It was evident that His main warfare was not to be against flesh and blood but against the 'spiritual hosts of wickedness in high places'. Here in the loneliness among the wild beasts Jesus battled for forty days with Satan. We are left to infer that He won a victory of potential importance for the rest of His ministry and for the subsequent history of mankind. Always Mark sees Jesus as the great victor over the demons. As He showed later in the case of the Gadarene swine and in the argument against those who accused Him of being in league with Beelzebub, Jesus possessed, and felt Himself to possess, a power which in the last resort the devils must always acknowledge.

Returning from the wilderness and taking up His mission Jesus meets with immediate success. The crowds throng Him. Attention is repeatedly drawn to their numbers and to His endeavours to escape their attentions (1^{45} 2^{13} $3^{7, 20-21}$). The impression He made was, in our current phrase, 'something out of this world'. People were astonished at His healings and at His power over the demons. Some however said He was mad. There was certainly more than a suggestion of the superhuman about Him. Even His nearest disciples, when they saw Him approaching their boat over the sea, thought He was a ghost. If, as this incident disclosed, His own followers were slow in grasping His true nature, the Jewish leaders were roused to complete antagonism. Against the developing opposition His numinous character comes out even more strongly. He remains a man of mystery to the end. There is something almost Wagnerian in the confusion of the night of His betrayal and the incident of the young man who escaped naked. The mystery culminates in the cry from the cross, 'My God, my God why didst thou forsake me?' with the darkness that preceded it and the tearing of the temple veil that followed it. The lesson is driven home by the verdict of the centurion 'Truly this man was a son of God'.

Amid all this suggestion of the *mysterium fascinans et tremendum* the writer never loses his touch with the ground. He recognises the challenge of the evil spirit 'I know thee' (1^{24}) as an attempt to resist dislodgment. He notices the similarity with flower beds in a garden when the crowd in their bright eastern robes sit down on 'the green grass' (6^{40}). He records the use of conventional means in the healing of the deaf and dumb man (7^{32-7}) and the gradualness of the healing in the case of the blind man (8^{22-6}). There is no straining after effect: the

THE FOUR PORTRAITS 177

supernatural element comes out simply because Mark feels it to be there. And it is there even on quite normal occasions. 'They were in the way going up to Jerusalem; and Jesus was going before them: and they were filled with awe; but some as they followed were afraid' (10^{32}). In his whole ministry Jesus is revealed as the mysterious Messiah.

III. THE UNIVERSAL HERO OF LUKE

St. Luke's view-point is rather different. It is not merely that he introduces much more of Christ's teaching, which he takes from Q and adds to Mark's narration, but that the use he makes of his own special source proclaims a rather different conception of Christ's figure. To St. Luke Jesus is not so much the martyred Messiah as the universal hero. As Luke is writing specifically for a Roman official it is natural that he should set his subject against the largest possible background. Consequently he traces Jesus' genealogy back to Adam (even to God!) and gives close attention to the historical setting of his story. Jesus' family is placed in its particular social group and we are given the most elaborate dating of the birth. This all smacks of the professional historian; and Luke must be given credit for his pains, although some modern scholars think that his narrative is the less valuable for having been so carefully worked over.

However that may be, the distinctive picture comes out all the more clearly. The mysterious element is for the most part omitted. The hero encounters opposition much earlier than we should have thought from Mark and His first public appearances in the town where He had been brought up nearly led to a lynching (Luke $4^{16\text{ff}}$.). Nevertheless we find Him soon making open proclamation of

His message in the so-called Sermon on the Plain. He shows particular interest in the poor and afflicted. He raises the widow's son at Nain, but reads a lesson in good manners to Simon, the wealthy Pharisee. He is ministered to by a number of faithful women and enjoys a comforting experience in the Transfiguration, which strengthens Him for the 'exodus' which is now seen to be the inevitable result of His mission.

Presently in the course of the story occurs the 'great insertion' (9^{51}–18^{14}) that Luke makes into the Marcan narrative. Here we have the mission and return of the Seventy, itself emphasising the importance of the leader; the parable of the Good Samaritan; the friendship with Lazarus and his family (cf. the Roman emphasis on friendship); the promise of the Kingdom to the 'little flock'; the defiant message to Herod; the stories to comfort the 'down-and-outs' such as the lost sheep, the lost coin and the lost son; the contrast between the respective fates of the rich man and the beggar, and finally the grateful Samaritan. All these fit the figure of the magnanimous leader.

They lead to an authoritative pronouncement on the approaching end of the world. St. Luke does not represent Jesus as having any great interest in apocalyptic speculation. Indeed He is described as warning his hearers against being panicked into a fear that the end was upon them (21^8). What is certain in Jesus' view is that Jerusalem itself is doomed to destruction. When they see the armies round the city they will be well advised to flee for refuge into the hills (21^{20}). How close to this will come the portents proclaiming the arrival of the Son of Man in the cloud does not appear, but Luke's view of the end is generally described as 'deferred eschatology'.

Jesus' special mixture of personal dignity and physical courage is maintained to the end. The Sanhedrin send Him to Pilate on the charge of claiming to be a king, and before Pilate He will not deny the charge. On the procession to Calvary He bids the Daughters of Jerusalem to weep for themselves rather than for Him. On the cross He first asks His Father's forgiveness for those who had brought Him to this ignominious death, then promises a place in His Kingdom to the penitent bandit, and at the last yields His soul calmly into His Father's hands. In a fitting final verdict the centurion declares that this must have been 'an innocent man'. Thus he expresses a Roman soldier's view that the Procurator had made a ghastly mistake in condemning Him. By this means Luke makes clear to his readers that Jesus, the Jewish religious hero, was not only the Messiah of His own people, proved to be such by His resurrection from the dead, or even the 'Lord of the Church's faith', but also a world-saviour of whom the great empire of Rome should take favourable notice.

More than any of the other evangelists Luke emphasises the kingly character of Jesus. He mentions the Kingdom even where Mark omits it; his songs refer back to the throne of David which the Messiah was to occupy (1^{69}); Jesus bequeathes His Kingdom to His apostles (22^{28}) and looks forward to sharing the Messianic banquet with them in that Kingdom (22^{18}). There is no contrast here between the 'Jesus of history' and the 'Christ of the Church'. The two are obviously identical. This is shown not by any dwelling on Pauline doctrines such as that of the kenosis or the atonement; nor even in the explicit statements of His supernatural character ($10^{21,22}$, 22^{69ff}.) It comes out naturally in the prophecies that He is to be the 'glory of Israel (2^{32}), in the experience of that glory in the Transfiguration and in the confirmation of it at the Ascension. This delineation has become so obvious to modern eyes that the current fashion is to number Luke, who hitherto had been regarded as *the* historian among New Testament writers *par excellence*, among those writers who are more interested in the interpretation than in the simple record of facts. Against the official Roman portrait of Jesus as a subversive pretender Luke sets clearly the picture of a saviour-king, one who suffered martyrdom for His belief in God and humanity.

IV. THE PRE-ORDAINED MESSIAH OF MATTHEW

If to Mark Jesus was a figure of awe and mystery, and to Luke a divine martyr-king, to Matthew He was the fulfilment of prophecy. The first evangelist was a more ecclesiastically minded person than any of the other three. He lived in the thought of the past and loved to find or invent parallels between God's dealings with His people in the ancient days and His revelation of Himself in Christ. It is the story of the Chosen People in which he is specially interested. So he traces Christ's genealogy only to Abraham, the first of the patriarchs; he dates events by reference to Herod, not to Roman officials (2^1); he arrives at an understanding of Christ's teaching by constant comparison with the ancient scriptures of his race; he makes the Sermon on the Mount (whether it is a single whole or a collection of fragments) appear like a proclamation of a new law to replace that given on Sinai; above all he loves to think that every action of Christ has been predicted long ago by the prophets, even though he is led into such oddities as applying Hosea's words, 'Out of Egypt have I called my son', to the flight of the holy family (2^{15}).

The Christ is shown to share the same interests as His

THE FOUR PORTRAITS 181

biographer. Consistently Jesus is depicted as a typical teacher or rabbi constantly recalling the past. It is in that spirit that He adjudicates on the Baptist, condemns the wicked cities, dilates on the mysteries of the Kingdom, clears up the law of the Sabbath, and insists on the payment of the temple tax. (All these incidents are recorded in chapters 11 to 17). He adjusts the relations of the new and the old Law; insists on recognition of the concern of the Church (or perhaps the local congregation) in any dispute between its members (18^{17}); and affirms the final victory of His Church (16^{18}). These are the only two references to the Church by that name (*ekklesia*) in the gospels, and it is significant that they appear in the narrative of this particular evangelist. There seems a deliberate reference to the old *ekklesia* or assembly of the people of God. Matthew is a great churchman.

If St. Matthew's gospel was really written for the Jews of Galilee, one would find it easy to understand the emphasis on the apocalyptic aspect of Christ's teaching, for apocalyptic was largely a Galilean interest, particularly common, it seems, in the immediate circle that formed Jesus' early environment. Even so it is notable how the end is referred back to the beginning. The careless lack of preparation will be like that before the Flood (24^{37}). It is from that point of reminiscence that the rest derives its spirit—the warning to watch, the doom pronounced on wicked servants, the parables of the ten virgins and of the talents (or 'bags of gold'), and the emphasis on simple morality as the criterion of judgment at the Last Day. Jesus is as conscious of the end as were the old apocalyptic prophets. But in the new the rhythm of the old is preserved: defection, suffering, repentance, rescue is still, as in the Old Testament, the recurrent cycle until the deliverance is made permanent in Christ.

Similarly when it comes to the betrayal by Judas and the purchase of the Potter's Field with the blood money, it is a prophecy from Jeremiah that is providentially fulfilled (27^{10}). The Jewish interest is further disclosed in Pilate's dramatic disclaimer of responsibility by the public washing of his hands. Thus the blame for the judicial murder is laid squarely on the shoulders of the Jewish leaders and is indeed accepted by them (27^{25}). These same leaders bring further shame on themselves by persuading Pilate to seal the tomb and so doubling their vain efforts to prevent even the semblance of a resurrection. As if to make clear that there was another side to current religion the risen Christ sends His disciples away from Jerusalem, the centre of official Judaism, and appears to them in Galilee, the home of many of them and the cradle of the new movement.

To Matthew then Jesus is the Messiah of prophecy, but it was a type of prophecy that yielded easily to apocalyptic visions. Two whole chapters (24 and 25) are devoted by Matthew to the subject.

V. THE WORD INCARNATE OF JOHN

In sharp contrast to these three pictures the author of the Fourth Gospel sees in Jesus mainly the Word Incarnate. He is no mere creature of time, whose genealogy can be satisfactorily traced back to Abraham or Adam: He is the projection into time of an eternal personality. The Jesus of John has no hesitation in ascribing divinity to Himself, 'I and my Father are one', nor does He object to others making the same claim for Him, as is implied in the detailed account of the forerunner's immediate recognition of His true character (1^{29-34}).

This description of Jesus is in line with the author's avowed purpose in composing his gospels, 'these things are written that you may believe that Jesus is the Christ, the Son of God, and that believing you may have life in His name'. This outspokenness about His apologetic purpose has led many commentators to think that John (if that be his real name) is only interested in interpretation and not in facts. In the past the designation of his writing as the 'spiritual' gospel has led to a sharp distinction between him and the synoptists. Today however while the difference is clearly seen, it is no longer regarded as a contradiction or even as a gravely distorting development. For this change of view there are two reasons; first the supernatural character of the Jesus presented to us even by the synoptic gospels is now generally recognised; and at the same time John is now given such credit for access to the actual facts of history that in some respects he is regarded as more accurate than the synoptists. The gap has thus been narrowed from either side.

It helps a good deal in attempting to understand the interpretation of the person of Christ given in the fourth gospel if we remember that the prologue sets the tone for everything that comes after. In Jesus of Nazareth John sees the eternal Logos using complete human nature through which to reveal, as fully as it can be revealed in humanity, the character of the Godhead. This is certainly an advance on the insight of the earlier gospels; but it is a natural advance: the Christian believer growing from the one to the other had nothing to unlearn.

It also helps to an understanding if we remind ourselves of the two opposite tendencies against which the author of the fourth gospel had to contend: that of Ebionism and that of Docetism, the one belittling the supernatural element in Christ and the other claiming that He was not a physical man at all but a phantom. Against these tendencies John affirms on the one hand that Jesus is true man, with a body so real that when the soldier pierced it with his spear there flowed out blood and water, the two constituent elements of human flesh. On the other hand He is also the very Son of God, sharing in the most distinctive of divine tasks, that of bestowing life: 'as the Father raises the dead and gives them life, so the Son gives life to men, as He determines' (5^{21}). Jesus is not only Lord but life-giver.

Perhaps the Christ depicted here has the closest affinities with the awe-inspiring figure of the Messiah of St. Mark's gospel. He has the same kind of effect on those brought in touch with Him. There is a temptation to think Him mad but even the soldiers sent to arrest him are compelled to say, 'No man ever spoke as this man speaks' (7^{46}).

One difficulty about the presentation in the Fourth Gospel is that little or no effort seems to have been made to hand on to us the *ipsissima verba* of Jesus. All the speeches have passed through the mind of the author; they are reported in his own style, and it is often difficult to tell where the words of the speaker end and those of the narrator begin. The differences between the parables of the synoptic gospels and the metaphors and analogies of the Fourth Gospel are well known. It is remarkable however, in spite of the literary contrasts, how clearly the portrait of Jesus appears: He is obviously the same person as is presented to us by the synoptists. This is largely because John sticks so closely to the physical facts of his narrative. If he had wished to 'spiritualise' the whole story and so make terms with the Gnostics, he would have had an excellent opportunity in rendering his account of the resurrection. But it is here more than anywhere that he asserts the actuality of the Lord's body, even in its risen form. By telling how Jesus pointed to the print of the nails he claims the identity of the one body, and proves it by the story of Thomas and his doubt ($20^{19\text{-}29}$).

In spite of this insistence on physical reality throughout the whole narrative, there is no concession to Ebionism. Jesus is truly divine. He is not only the Word, but also the Way, the Truth and the Life and claims to be one with the Father. There are two sides to the shield of His existence, and you cannot have the one without the other. But in this double character He is not completely isolated. Just as He is God and man, so all physical things are capable of being made the vehicles of spiritual reality. John's view of the incarnation leads straight into a sacramental view of all existence. Physical events are 'signs', tangible symbols of an intangible truth. Jesus is not merely 'like' certain material things, He *is* their real essence. He is not a copy of them, but they of Him. He is the real vine, the real light, the real road. None of these physical realities could exist if He were not in the eternal sphere already what they represent, and indeed, in a secondary and temporary sense, actually are in the material world. So it is possible for Him to give His own flesh and blood for food. The bread and wine He has designated for the purpose become His flesh and blood, the vehicles of His actual personality, and can make such faithful believers as partake of them sharers in that personality. Again, this is an advance on what the synoptists have told us, but it seems so easily compatible with their account that we are led to conclude merely that the writer of this gospel penetrated more deeply into the mind of the Master than did they.

If correct interpretation of established fact is the major part of the historian's task, then there is some justification for regarding the fourth evangelist as the best historian of them all. In any case it is clear that without his distinctive portrait of Christ our knowledge of Jesus would be greatly impoverished.

We are indeed fortunate in having four pictures, so independently drawn, in spite of considerable common material. If sometimes we are struck by what seems a marked dissimilarity between one and another, that is no more than we should expect today if we were examining the proofs of photographs freshly taken of some one near to us whom we know well. How often are we tempted to say, 'Well, I could hardly have believed it was the same person.' Yet our knowledge of the person's appearance is immensely enriched if we are able to see him in a number of pictures taken from different points of view.

CHAPTER XV

SUMMARY AND CONCLUSION

1. FINAL ESTIMATE

IT is customary at the end of a biography to present some estimate of the work and character of one's hero. Normally this is the most valuable part of the book. It helps us to make some general estimate of the subject of our portrait and to draw some conclusion as to his importance in the history of his own and subsequent times. Such a task, however rewarding, is never easy. It presupposes on the part of the writer a capacity to stand away from the events he has been recording and to judge their influence from outside, like a general reviewing his troops and taking the salute from the vantage point of an exalted dais. This is never completely possible because none of us is entirely outside the march of history. We are ourselves in the ranks even while we try in imagination to stand by the side of the commanding officer.

In the case of Jesus the task is incomparably more difficult. For Christians Jesus is no mere figure of the historic past. He is also the cosmic Christ, the agent both in the original creation of the universe and of its ultimate judgment. Indeed the laws by which it is sustained are but the expression of His will. When Canon Streeter, one of the ablest New Testament scholars we have had in modern times, was trying to evaluate the message of the Fourth Gospel, he was constrained to preface his essay with a quotation from Plunkett:

> I see His blood upon the rose,
>   And in the stars the glory of His eyes;
> His body gleams amid eternal snows,
>   His tears fall from the skies.

It is obvious that one writing from such a point of view cannot give a cold, dispassionate judgment of the historical figure from which the picture of the incarnate Christ purports to be drawn. His emotions are already too much involved.

In listening to agnostics arguing about Jesus of Nazareth one is sometimes taken aback by finding that they are unwilling to concede that He displays even human character in its perfection. They will instance the Gadarene swine, the barren fig-tree, the forcible cleansing of the Temple as examples of inconsiderateness, petulance or narrow-mindedness. Or they will complain of Jesus' lack of interest in economics and politics as exhibiting a failure in good citizenship. The Christian may retort that in each particular case the objectors have misunderstood either the record or the necessities of the time. But his real defence is that, accepting Jesus as the perfect revelation of God in human nature, he would rather suspend judgment where he cannot for the moment understand. He is like the tourist in the National Gallery. He is not there to judge the masterpieces: they are the standard by which he himself must be judged.

Nevertheless we must exercise at least a tentative criticism in order that our taste may be trained and we may learn to appreciate the highest standards. As historians we must make sure of our facts and understand both the environment of our subject and the impression He made upon it. As religious enquirers into

SUMMARY AND CONCLUSION 189

the life of Jesus we shall have faith to believe that the more we know the more profound will be our adoration.

II. PERSONAL POWER

The impression of Jesus gained by His contemporaries was certainly not that of the weak and languishing figure of later imagination. He was above all a man of power. One who could induce grown men to give up their trade and join His crusade, who could calm the hysterical and be credited with the stilling of a storm, who could dominate the crowds and reduce professional hecklers to silence was certainly no weakling. Indeed power flowed from Him in such abundance that it could galvanise His immediate friends into a similar display of dynamic personality. The main evidence that the Kingdom of Heaven had already begun on earth was seen in this sudden access of creative activity manifested in Jesus and His immediate circle. This impression can still be gained by those who make a fresh and unsentimental approach to the original records. How strongly it can still affect the non-theological layman can be seen by anyone who will read Dr. E. V. Rieu's introduction to his new translation of the Four Gospels in the *Penguin Classics*.

Dr. Rieu collects the indications he has found in the original Greek of the personal traits of Jesus—the flashing eyes, the powerful frame, the long stride that carried Him ahead of His disciples, the strong voice, the witty repartee, the learning and the literary ability, the quiet humour, the ruthless self-discipline. To this we can add the gentleness that is so especially attractive in a strong man, the love of nature and of children, the combined humility and authority of the born teacher.

As a boy Jesus had shown a marked independence of character together with a ready obedience to His parents. As a man, even upon the Cross, He was the protector of His mother. He was a leader who combined the sternest demands upon His followers with the tenderest care of the sick and suffering whether in body or in mind.

As a speaker He deliberately eschewed the arts of the demagogue. It is true that He took infinite pains to pierce to the conscience of His hearers and to produce the kind of conviction that issues in action. Yet He would never inflame passion, and as soon as excitement was aroused He would retire into temporary obscurity until it had died down. It has often been pointed out how He would make statements even about Himself that seemed on a superficial view to be contradictory. Nowhere does that come out more clearly than in the Fourth Gospel, where His announcement 'For judgment I am come into this world'[1] is balanced by the disclaimer 'I judge no man.'[2] Although He had come to save the whole world He would allow no missionary enterprise in His own time outside the ranks of Israel, leaving the apparent contradiction to be reconciled within the spreading boundaries of the Kingdom of God. He would allow intending disciples to leave Him rather than whittle away what He had said about the necessity of 'eating His flesh and drinking His blood'. In any age it must require a specially strong character to teach by contraries rather than by the 'nicely calculated less or more'.

The advantage of an educational method that refuses to produce cut and dried answers to every question is that it forces the learners to think for themselves. The fact that it also leaves room for difference of opinion

[1] Jn. 9^{39}. [2] Jn. 8^{15}.

must be taken as inevitable. Both consequences are specially obvious in connection with the doctrine of the Messiah. In modern times it has been possible for scholars of renown to doubt whether Jesus claimed to be the Messiah at all. The undoubted claim made on His behalf in the gospels is put down to the fancy of the early Church. Happily the greater weight of modern scholarship accepts the verisimilitude of the picture presented by the evangelists, and we can be content to ask ourselves, as Jesus taught His disciples to ask, precisely what He meant by His claim to Messiahship.

In all probability our Lord's contemporaries understood by the Messiah some kind of national leader after the pattern of King David. A part of that expectation was undoubtedly the restoration of independent sovereignty to Israel. The picture had been idealised through the influence of the glowing descriptions in the Prophets of the enhanced fruitfulness of nature in the Messianic Age. This was the foundation upon which Jesus had to build. He eliminated the exclusively nationalist and political elements and substituted for them the idea of a Kingdom in which the rule of God would be acknowledged and obeyed both by society and the individual, and in which Israel would fulfil the ancient promise that she should be a means of blessing for the whole of mankind.

This idea of a David *redivivus* had been crossed in the apocalyptic circles of Judaism by the idea of a Son of Man who in the extremity of His people would be sent by God from Heaven to deliver the nation and inflict vengeance on its enemies. There is some doubt whether this Son of Man was conceived as an individual, or as a corporate entity representing the ideal Israel, or as the martyred saints of the nation returning in glory. In any case it is more than probable that Jesus applied this conception to Himself. He took the title Son of Man, implying that He was actually sent from Heaven to rescue Israel. The apocalyptic picture of a descent from Heaven in glory for the purposes of judgment He transferred to a second coming in which He would pass sentence, not on Israel's enemies, but on evil wherever it should be found whether in Israel or among the Gentiles.

A third element in Jesus' conception of Messiahship is unique, at least in the sense that no one is known to have employed it in this connection before. This is the idea of the Suffering Servant, taken from the songs of 'Isaiah' of which the 53rd chapter is the best known. The idea conveyed in these poems is that the nation will in the last resort be 'redeemed' not by force of arms but by the vicarious suffering and undeserved death of one who is at once the servant of the people and the servant of Jehovah. Here again it is not certain whether the 'servant' is an individual or a 'remnant' of the people or an ideal Israel. There can in any case be no doubt[1] that Jesus applied the thought to Himself. It is obvious that the incorporation of this conception into the Messianic expectation was quite revolutionary. Israel was to be saved not by conquest but by suffering: her deliverer was to achieve his end not by victory in battle but by death. This was in itself sufficient to involve a complete re-writing of the current Messianic expectation. The positive aim of Jesus' teaching on the subject was to induce His disciples to look at the Messiahship from this point of view. They seem to have been quite incapable of entering into His mind in this respect, and it was not until after His Resurrection that they under-

[1] But see M. D. Hooker, *Jesus and the Servant* (S.P.C.K., 1959).

stood the relevance of His teaching. Then at last it became part of their own apologia, and thus it became possible to claim that the Passion and Crucifixion were part of God's ordained plan for the salvation of the world.

III. SON OF GOD

The term Son of Man, whether it means Archetypal Man or Messiah, or is just used as a periphrasis for the first person singular pronoun, seems to have been Jesus' favourite title for Himself. There is, however, much in the gospels to make clear the fact that both in His own view about Himself and in the early tradition of His followers Jesus was more than man.

In Hellenistic circles there was no such hard and fast distinction between humanity and divinity as appears axiomatic to ourselves. Gods might bear human children and heroes might be deified. Jews, however, did not entertain such ideas. To them there was only one God, Jehovah, and all other existences were His creatures. It is one of the miracles of human thought that men brought up in such an atmosphere could nevertheless come to accept Jesus as divine. The ascription to Him of the title *Kyrios* or Lord, which is so prominent in Luke, and which in the Septuagint is so often applied to Jehovah Himself, shows how the bridge could be built.

Naturally it is the title Son of God, much favoured by Mark, which seems to us to be most directly indicative of Jesus' divinity. Not that the phrase necessarily and in every instance implies divine status. In the Old Testament it is applied to the King or the nation. In such cases it does not suggest sonship by birth, but by adoption. We should naturally expect that it would be particularly applicable to the Messiah, but there appears to be no instance of such usage in pre-Christian Judaism. In the Synoptics, however, that identification is clear both in the declaration of St. Peter and in the trial before the Sanhedrin.[1] There is even an advance on this. It is probable that all three synoptists feel that more than Messiahship is implied in the use of the title Son by the divine voice at Jesus' baptism and transfiguration. 'This is My beloved Son' implies a quite unique status. In any case both Matthew and Luke show by their narratives of the wondrous birth that Jesus is in a unique sense the Son of God.

It is in the Fourth Gospel that the implications of the title Son are brought out most clearly. Other people might ascend from the lower to the higher status by being adopted as sons of God, but in Jesus the reverse process was seen. He was the Logos incarnate and as such He came down from God out of eternity into time, and after a sojourn as man among men would return to 'the things above'. True, He was absolutely dependent upon His Father, but He was one with the Father and all divine powers were given to Him. He knew God and could fully reveal Him. He was both life-giver and judge. He shared the Father's glory before the beginning of the world and would resume it after the days of His humiliation were over. Even before the birth of Abraham He shared Jehovah's title 'I am'.[2]

IV. CONCLUSION

This brings us back to the point from which we started at the opening of this book. It is in the last resort impossible to write a life of Jesus Christ without

[1] Mt. 16^{16}, 26^{63}, Mk. 14^{61}.
[2] C. H. Dodd, *Interpretation of Fourth Gospel*, pp. 250-62. C.U.P.

SUMMARY AND CONCLUSION

making it clear whether you believe Him to be the Son of God or not. Many attempts are spoilt because the underlying presuppositions with which the author starts are not laid bare. But everyone has some presuppositions and it seems more fair to the reader to let them be known. Those who start with the belief that 'miracles do not happen' or that Jesus was merely 'a man like other men' will inevitably reject as poetic symbolism or legendary accretion much that has here been accepted as sober fact.

It is no part of our present task to prove the divinity of Jesus Christ. That belongs to the sphere of Christian apologetics. All we need do here is to repeat that the facts as far as we have been able to discover them are not inconsistent with that doctrine. At any rate that was certainly the belief of the evangelists and other early Christian writers. Modern scholars have done a great deal to explore the period between the actual life of Jesus and the earliest Christian documents. They have been able to show, what indeed we knew already, that belief in Jesus was the result of a gradual realisation of the meaning of His life and work. But they have not been able to show either that He did not make the strongest claims for Himself or that the early Church refused to accept those claims. In other words the modern reader is in the same position as the evangelists. We can understand the life of Jesus only from this point of view. In this way and in no other does it appear to make sense. When we think of Jesus the Christ we are moved to admiration for the hero, to love for the friend, but above all, like the early disciple who was something of a rationalist in his day, to adoration for the numinous quality which wrings from us the final cry, 'My Lord and my God.'

FOR FURTHER READING

Books on this subject are legion, but the reader who wishes to make a further study on modern lines might well begin with the following:

Jesus, Son of Man. G. S. Duncan. (Nisbet, 1947.)

The Work and Words of Jesus. A. M. Hunter. (S.C.M., 1950.)

Jesus, Master and Lord.[1] H. E. W. Turner. (Mowbray, 1953.)

Jesus of Nazareth. Günther Bornkamm. (Hodder & Stoughton, 1960.)

[1] This gives admirable bibliographies at the end of each chapter.

INDEX

'Abomination of Desolation', 141–2
Abraham, 21, 178
Acts of the Apostles, 3
Adam, 21
S. Andrew, 49, 50, 57, 63, 139–40, 141
Annas, 153
Annunciation, 16, 22
Antiochus Epiphanes, 35
Apocalypse, 16, 141–2, 176
Apocalyptists, the, 14, 39, 142
Apocrypha, 69
Apocryphal Gospels, 13, 130
Apostles, the Twelve, 62–4, 83, 99, 100, 108, 121, 126, 133
Ascension, 24, 170
Atonement, 97, 131

Baptism, 9, 44–7, 53, 87
Barabbas, 156
Barren Fig-tree, incident of the, 133–5, 172
Bartimaeus, 121
Bath-Qol ('Voice from Heaven'), 46, 87, 140
Beatitudes, 64, 95
Bethany, 119, 122, 133, 135, 141, 143, 170
Bethesda, 10, 59
Bethlehem, 26–8
Bultmann, Professor, 15, 17

Caesarea Philippi 84, 96, 102
Caiaphas, 120, 144, 153
Cana, 51, 56, 101
Capernaum, 50, 54, 57–8, 61, 83, 88
Christianity, contemporary accounts of, 3–5; as 'myth', 15–17; as religion of Jesus Christ, 101
Church, the, 5, 34, 41, 83, 97, 99–100, 128, 164, 170, 179
Circumcision, 29
Crucifixion, 6, 52, 157–60

David, 21, 27, 71, 132, 135, 175
Dedication, Feast of, 53, 115
Dispersion, Jews of the, 35–6
Dodd, Professor, 74–5

Egypt, Flight into, 28, 30
Elijah, 59, 84, 86
Emmaus, 166–7
Essenes, 38

Five Thousand, feeding of the, 81
Four Thousand, feeding of the, 82

Gabriel, 16
Galilee, 38–9, 41–2, 50, 52, 54, 55, 57, 60, 61, 82, 83, 88, 92, 155, 161, 166, 168–9
Gentiles, 38, 64, 65, 82, 116, 119, 139, 140
Gethsemane, 151–3, 154, 158
Golgotha, 157, 159
Good Friday, 157–61
Greek Philosophy, 34–5, 72

Herod Antipas, 36, 60–1, 80, 117, 155–6
Herod the Great, 21, 25, 28, 36, 45, 140

Herodians, 37, 137
Herodias, 60-1, 80

Incarnation, 6, 16, 17, 128

S. James, 50, 57, 85, 89, 91, 141, 151
Jerusalem, 27, 29, 30, 35, 36, 38, 40, 52, 54, 59, 60, 89, 90, 91, 115, 117, 119-21, 131-4, 142, 144, 155, 161, 167, 169
Joad, Professor, 129-30
S. John, son of Zebedee, 49, 50, 57, 85, 89, 91, 141, 147, 148, 151, 154, 158, 160, 165, 168
S. John's Gospel ('the Fourth Gospel'), 6-7, 10-11, 20, 47, 49, 50, 53, 54-6, 60, 70-1, 82, 94, 99, 103, 104, 120, 126, 127, 135, 146, 150, 171, 174
S. John the Baptist, 44-7, 55, 57, 60-1, 79-81, 84, 103, 106, 110, 116, 117, 125, 135, 136
S. Joseph, 21, 22, 24, 26-8, 43
Joseph of Arimathea, 160-1
Josephus, 4, 25, 28, 80-1, 89, 114
Judaea, 38, 44, 55, 120, 170
Judaism, 40-2, 133, 135, 142, 175
Judas Iscariot, 63, 122, 144, 148, 151, 152, 154-5

Kingdom of Heaven, 64, 72, 94, 96-9, 100, 106-7, 110, 112, 113, 116, 118, 124, 128, 143, 150, 173

Last Supper, 99, 103
Lazarus, 11, 119-20, 127

Lord's Prayer, 110-11
S. Luke's Gospel, 7-9, 11, 12, 21, 22, 24, 25, 27, 29-30, 45, 47, 50, 52, 57, 58, 64-6, 77-8, 79, 87, 109, 111, 142, 155, 169, 177-8

Magi, the, 23, 27
Marcus Aurelius, 34
S. Mark, 147, 153
S. Mark's Gospel, 7-9, 11, 12, 20, 46, 47, 50, 52, 77-8, 82, 83, 123, 142, 146, 169, 177
Martha, 119, 122
Mary Magdalene, 164-6
Mary, Mother of Jesus Christ, 16, 21, 24, 26-30, 42
Mary of Bethany, 119, 122
S. Matthew, 61-2, 63, 79, 82, 83, 89
S. Matthew's Gospel, 7-9, 11, 20, 21, 24, 27, 28, 47, 50, 52, 63, 64-5, 77-8, 84, 95, 99, 109, 111, 112, 142, 155, 159, 162, 169
Maundy Thursday, 146-56
Messiah, Jesus Christ as, 1, 20, 21, 22, 28, 29-30, 42, 47-9, 53, 58, 63, 82, 84-5, 96, 99, 102, 115, 120, 132, 153, 158, 170, 175-6
Miracles, 111-12, 123-30; at Cana, 51, 56, 101; at Capernaum, 58, 61, 65; at Bethesda, 59; widow of Nain, 65-6, 124; feeding of the Five Thousand, 81; walking on the water, 83; healing of the epileptic boy, 87-8; at Samaria, 91; at the pool of Siloam, 11, 92; raising of Lazarus, 119-20, 127; healing of Bartimaeus, 121-2
Moses, 86, 95, 139
Mount of Olives, 151, 170

INDEX

Nathaniel, 50, 56
Nativity, the, 24–9
Nazareth, 28–30, 39, 50, 58, 65, 125, 133, 152
Nero, 3
New Testament, 17, 19, 23, 39, 41, 100, 127, 130, 164
Nicodemus, 54–6, 160

Old Testament, 21, 22, 29, 35, 39, 41, 69, 71, 79, 99, 177

Palestine, 33–6
Palm Sunday, 131–3
Parables, 68–78; of the Hidden Treasure, 73; of the Ten Virgins, 74, 143; of the Sower, 74–5; of the Unjust Steward, 75; of the Lost Sheep, 77, 118; of the Lost Coin, 77, 118; of the Prodigal Son, 77, 101, 102, 118, 138; of the Good Samaritan, 109; of the Rich Fool, 113; of the Wicked Husbandmen, 138; of the Wedding Feast, 139; of the Talents, 143; of the Sheep and the Goats, 143
Passion of Our Lord, 9, 53, 86, 131–45
Passover, 10, 30, 52, 53, 54, 59, 119, 122, 146, 149, 160
S. Paul, 5, 13, 24, 83, 97, 150, 169
Pentecost, 10, 53
'People of the Land', 41–2
Perea, 52, 61, 116, 119
S. Peter, 53, 58, 83, 84, 85, 86, 88, 90, 96, 99, 102, 113, 141, 147, 148, 151, 152, 154, 165, 167, 168, 178
Pharisees, 37, 41, 54, 61–2, 66, 109, 112–13, 116–18, 120, 125, 132, 138, 139, 161–2

S. Philip, 50, 63, 139–40
Pliny, 4
Pontius Pilate, 4, 36, 114, 155–7, 160

'Q', 8–9, 12, 47, 64–5, 79, 111, 112
Quebec, Archbishop of, 11–12
Questions, Day of, 135–43
Quirinius, 25, 36

Rabbis, 4, 21, 31, 39, 41, 46, 76, 95, 110, 137, 138, 152
Resurrection, 24, 128, 163–70

Sabbath, the, 10, 60, 62, 91, 117, 161
Sadducees, 37
Samaria, 38, 55, 90, 170
Samaritans, 56, 64, 91, 109, 114
Sanhedrin, 37, 54, 62, 92, 120, 153, 155, 160
Satan, 16, 108, 111, 125
Schweitzer, Albert, 14, 105–6
Scribes, 37, 58
Seely, Sir John, 14
Septuagint, the, 35, 70, 177
Sermon on the Mount, 64, 95, 104, 109
Sermon on the Plain, 64
Siloam, 11, 92
Simeon, 42, 50
Simon of Cyrene, 157
Simon the Zealot, 57, 63
Simon the Pharisee, 66, 76
Simon the Leper, 122, 131, 144
Son of God, Jesus Christ as, 15, 24, 26, 46, 48, 84, 100–102, 164, 177–9
Son of Man, Jesus Christ as, 15, 102, 175–7

Suetonius, 3
Suffering Servant, songs of the, 85, 102–3, 132, 176
Synoptic Gospels, 6–12, 94, 133, 146, 178

Tabernacles, Feast of, 10, 53, 90–2, 108
Tacitus, 3
Teacher, Jesus Christ as, 93–6
Temple, the, 29, 30, 36, 48, 98, 115, 133–5, 136–41, 143, 148, 153, 154, 159; tax, 88–9, 134, 137

Temptation, 9, 16, 47–9, 54, 112
Thomas, 120, 167
Transfiguration, 9, 53, 87

Virgin Birth, 22, 24

Word of God (Logos), 7, 14, 20, 26, 178

Zacchaeus, 121
Zealots, 38, 63

For Product Safety Concerns and Information please contact our EU representative GPSR@taylorandfrancis.com
Taylor & Francis Verlag GmbH, Kaufingerstraße 24, 80331 München, Germany

www.ingramcontent.com/pod-product-compliance
Lightning Source LLC
Chambersburg PA
CBHW061445300426
44114CB00014B/1842